Home Distillation Handbook

How to distil quality alcohol at home inexpensive and safely

By Ola Norrman

Internet publishing
Bokforlaget Exakt, Malmo, Sweden

Photo setting
Bokforlaget Exakt, Malmo, Sweden

Illustrations
Tord Haegg, Malmo, Sweden

Graphic design & Illustrations
Jonathan Cowen

Printed by
Bokforlaget Exakt in Malmo, Sweden 2015

This book is also worldwide available as a
Kindle book at Amazon.

Please note that it is illegal to put to practical use
the contents of this book in certain countries. However home
distillation is a good talking point, and acquiring such
knowledge is an easy burden.

© Bokforlaget Exakt, Box 50221, 202 12 Malmo, Sweden.

ISBN 9781512188530

Contents

Copyright and Internet	6
Introduction	7
Natural Home Distillation	8
Equipment for fermentation	9
Fermentation vessel	9
Fermentation lid	10
Rubber plug (Bung)	11
Rubber caps	11
Fermentation lock	12
The Siphon	13
Measuring	14
The Hydrometer (with Oechslescale)	14
Hydrometer Instructions	15
Measuring glass for the alcometer and hydrometer	15
Alcometer	16
Laboratory Thermometer	17
Distillation Apparatus	18
The Still	18
Distillation column filling	20
Counter-flow rinsing of column	22
Heat source for the still	22
The Thermometer	23
Electronic Temperature Control	24
There are two reliable solutions that function well	25
The LAB MASTER distilling apparatus	26
The boiling vessel	27
Material	28
Austenitic stainless steel or copper	28
Thermometer connection point	29
As viewed from base of column	30

Mounting of column filling Retention strip	30
Fixing of column filling retention plate	31
Circulation of cooling water	31
Ingredients	33
Quantities	33
METRIC / USA / UNITED KINGDOM	33
CONVERSION	33
Water	34
Sugar	34
Yeast	34
Yeast Nutrients	35
Turbo Yeast	36
Clearing Agents (Finings)	37
Activated Carbon	38
Activated carbon is always active	40
How much activated carbon is used?	40
Aquarium charcoal	41
Deposits in the spirit	41
Essences	42
The advantages of essences	46
Literature about home distilling	48
Where to buy essences:	49
Mash fermentation	50
Preparing the mash	50
How much sugar is required?	52
Purer fermentation with Turbo Yeast	54
Turbo Yeast	55
Some Turbo Yeasts and their characteristics	56
A note about whisky and fruit schnapps	58
Basic instructions:	59
What makes for a "good" Turbo?	59
The key to making world-class spirits and liqueurs in the home	59

Understanding the science of fermentation	60
Yeast is a living organism	61
All about temperature	62
There are 3 types of temperature we need to talk about:	62
Some different quality Turbos	63
Turbo Yeast instructions for 25 Litres	64
Some words about quality	66
A last trick to improve quality	66
Large volume fermentation	67
Instructions for large volume fermentation	68
Mash fermentation with Turbo Yeast	70
Mash fermentation with baker´s yeast	72
Distillation	74
Pressure	74
Re-distillation	75
Fractional distillation	76
How to distil extra pure alcohol	78
The Amazing Method	79
Temperature	80
Effect of atmospheric pressure on boiling points	80
Theoretical thresholds in a distillation column	81
The actual location of the thresholds	81
Distillation procedure	82
SAFETY: Danger of accidents and other important points	**84**
Explosions	85
Risk of fire	86
Flooding	87
Poisoning	87
Trouble shooting - Distillation fails to start	**88**
Dilution	90
Fusel oil - Facts about fusel oil	**91**
Purification using activated carbon	92
Procedure	93

Activated Carbon Filtration Unit	**96**
Purification using the same activated carbon twice	96
Purification must be perfect	97
Different brands of activated carbon	97
Blending with essences	98
Basic prerequisites:	98
Blending with spirit essences	100
Blending with liqueur essences	100
Formula for calculating dilution	101
Table of original alcohol content of liqueurs	102
Original gravity of liqueurs	103
Original gravity of aperitifs and bitters	103
Legislation - **Freedom of the press**	**104**
It is obvious	104
Punishment	105
Is the law wrong in your country?	105
Internet Links -	
Here are some great links for the Internet.	**106**
Notes:	108

Copyright and Internet

Reproduction of the contents of this book, in whole or part is forbidden, and is a breach of the Law of Copyright without the express permission of the author. Neither is it permitted to reproduce figures or illustrations and applies to all forms of reproduction, by copying, printing, duplicating, stenciling, tape recording, etc. This also includes copies of this book downloaded from the Internet.

© Bokforlaget Exakt, Box 50221,
202 12 Malmo, Sweden.

Introduction

The law of freedom of information makes it possible to publish this book. The practices described in this book are still illegal in Sweden and in many other countries, and what "one" does in this book is not intended to tempt the reader. But knowledge is an easy burden and amateur distillation is free in several countries. Pleasant reading!

The Author

PS

I would again like to stress that the contents of this book are not intended to encourage the reader to break the law. If it is illegal in your country to distil alcohol you should naturally not do so. This book describes the technical aspects of home distillation as it is practiced in countries where it is legal.

Natural Home Distillation

Natural home distillation comprises mash fermentation followed by distillation and after-treatment. This can be split up into the following stages:

* Equipment

* Ingredients

* Fermentation

* Distillation

* Dilution

* Purification

* Flavouring

Natural home distillation has been a tradition for many hundreds of years in Sweden. Domestic distillation has been taxed at various times, allowed or forbidden since the sixteen hundreds. Currently home distillation is forbidden and the processes covered by this book are illegal in Sweden. However, knowledge is not a heavy burden and home distillation is allowed in many countries of the world today.

Equipment for fermentation

Fermentation vessel

One of the best fermentation vessels for mash is a wine-making container. These are graduated from 1 to 30 Litres (or in pints and gallons) and the graduation is very useful. The lid is removable so that sugar can be dissolved directly in the water. The vessel is wide at the top so that the carbon dioxide leaves at the widest point, which speeds up fermentation. Such vessels are very easy to keep clean.

The next most useful type is a polythene container (a water container of the type used for camping) and approved for containing foodstuffs. This type of container is easier to handle than a glass demijohn and is much less fragile.

Fermentation lid

Lids or caps are available for plastic containers. They screw on and are provided with a hole and rubber grommet for the fermentation lock. These covers are not recommended. They often leak or leak after a time. Conical rubber plugs provided with a hole for the fermentation lock are better as they never leak.

Rubber plug (Bung)

A rubber plug is better than a lid or rubber cap for plastic containers. A rubber plug (bung) never allows carbon dioxide to escape from around the fermentation lock. Larger rubber plugs are available for glass demijohns. These are good but often several times more expensive than rubber caps. Rubber plugs (bungs) last 2-3 times longer than rubber caps.

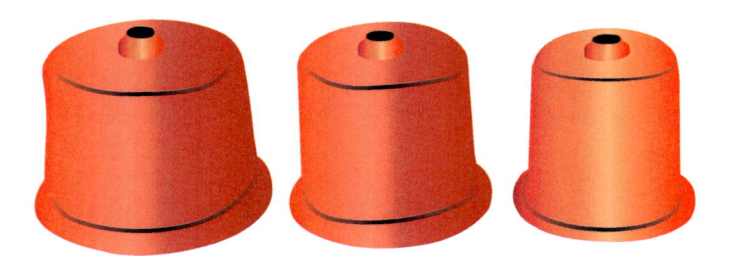

Rubber caps

A rubber cap does not leak between glass demijohns and the fermentation lock. However, note that rubber caps leak if they are used on plastic containers. Even if they are sealed with wire or jubilee clips leakage will occur. It is suggested to use food grade bungs if possible.

Fermentation lock

The fermentation lock should be of plastic. It contains a water trap that allows the venting of carbon dioxide but prevents the fermentation coming into contact with air.

When fermenting with Turbo Yeast or other rapid fermenting yeast your fermentation lock should not be used for the first few days. Fermentation will be so violent that the water will be forced out.

The carbon dioxide, which is heavier than air, protects the fermentation from air. The fermentation lock should be fitted when the violent fermentation has subsided.

There is a fermentation lock that is odour free at partymanshop.com/fermentation-lock-odor-free.html and is also available at allfreightfree.com. This fermentation lock has water to keep the air out, and activated carbon to absorb the odour. When the activated carbon, that is enclosed, is used up you can use the same activated carbon that is used for alcohol purification.

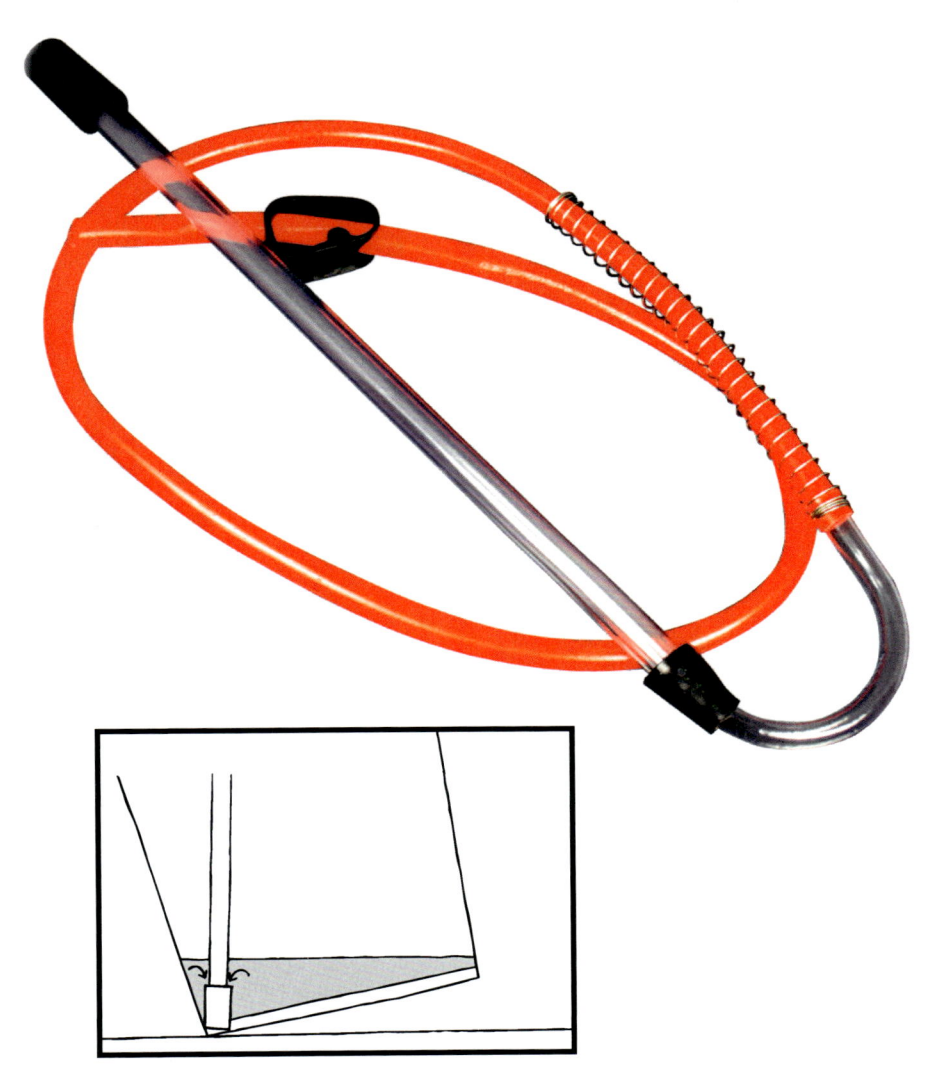

The Siphon

Siphons should be plastic. Siphons made from rubber tubes often cause off tasting flavours if used for alcohol. The siphon is used for transferring the finished mash. The mash is transferred to the still but is designed to leave the yeast deposit behind. The siphon leaves about 20 mm of deposit behind in the fermentation vessel.

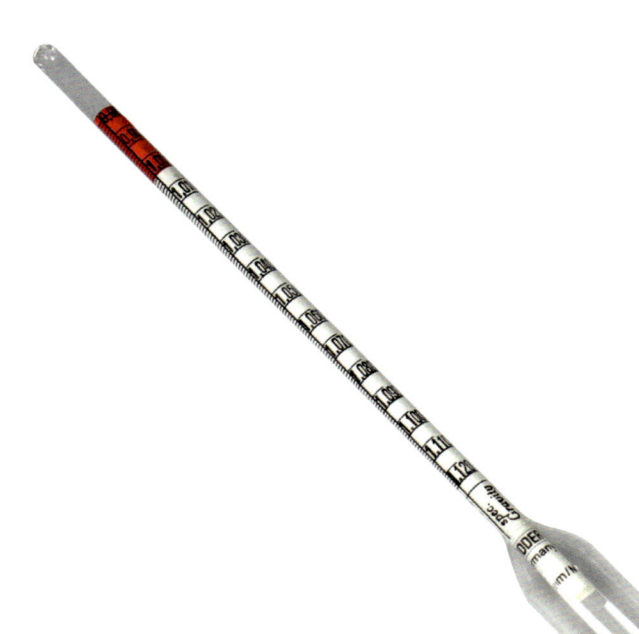

Measuring

The Hydrometer (with Oechslescale)

The Hydrometer indicates when fermentation has ceased in the mash. When the instrument shows -10° to -20° Oechsle (spec. gravity 0.980-0.990) or below (in the coloured field) the fermentation is complete.

Fermentation usually starts at +80° (spec. gravity 1.080) or higher. The hydrometer should be 300 mm long. It should be free floating, and read at the surface of the liquid. (Rather like checking the specific gravity of battery electrolyte).

The hydrometer is the only way of determining that the mash fermentation has ceased. It is no indication when the bubbling from the fermentation lock ceases, as carbon dioxide can be leaking from somewhere.

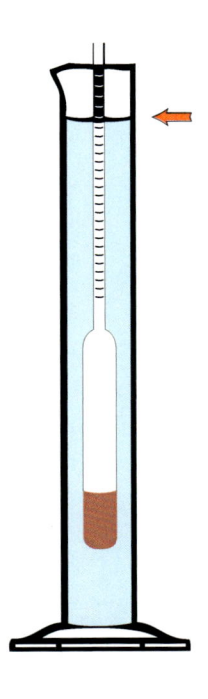

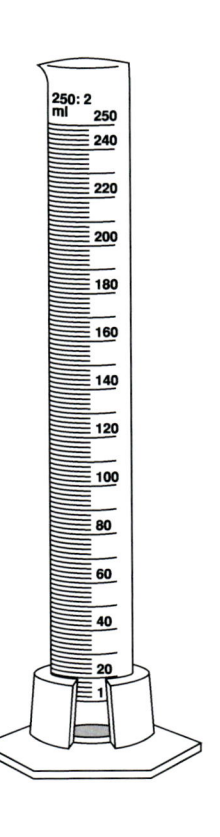

Hydrometer Instructions

Allow the hydrometer to float freely and read off from the surface of the liquid. If one wants to know the alcoholic content of the mash the hydrometer must be used.

The hydrometer temperature (in degrees), minus the starting temperature, divided by 8 = the percentage of alcohol by volume.

Example: Starting value = 80° (white field) and final value -16° (coloured field). Finished fermentation reading is 80° on the plus scale and 16° on the minus scale, giving 96 degrees. 96 divided by 8 =12%, which is the alcohol in the mash. If the hydrometer is graduated in specific gravity
+80° Oechsle = 1.080, -16° Oechsle = 0.984. Complete hydrometer info on-line at www.thehydrometer.com.

Measuring glass for the alcometer and hydrometer

Assuming one has a 250 or 300 mm instrument, a measuring glass is best. For a 250 mm instrument a 100 ml high glass is best, and for a 300 mm a 250 ml high glass is suitable.

With a measuring glass it is not necessary to use so much spirits, and the glass will be the correct height.

The measuring glass should be graduated in millilitres so that it can also be used for measuring volume. With an alcoholmeter and a measuring glass much mixing and measuring can be carried out. Refer to sections covering dilution, essences, tables, etc.

Alcometer

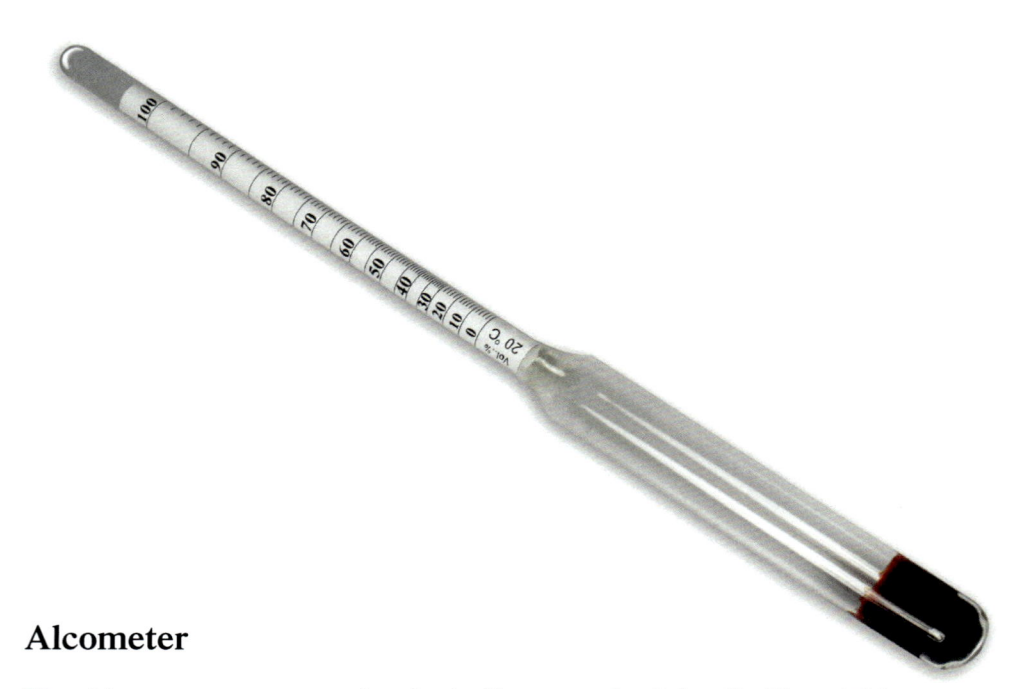

The Alcometer measures the alcoholic strength of the distillate. This functions only in pure mixtures of alcohol and water. It is graded from 0 to 100% - there are also some other scales.

The alcohol metre functions in the same way as a hydrometer, it should be allowed to float in the spirits. The reading is on the surface of the spirits, like with a battery tester.

The longer the instrument is the more accurate it will read. One should not be satisfied with less than a laboratory model of 250 to 300 mm long.

These have an accuracy of +-1%, whereas the shorter models of 150 mm can give a reading which is up to 10% wrong. In the case of the short instruments the graduation is so fine that it is very difficult to read when showing fewer than 50%. The alcohol metre shows the alcoholic content by volume. Instruments are available that are extremely accurate with a scale between 30 and 60%.

One model also comes with a thermometer with a correction scale. Alcometers are only accurate at exactly 20°C. So for complete accuracy an alcometer with a thermometer and correction scale must be used.

Laboratory Thermometer

The most important task for the thermometer is to determine the temperature at the top of the column during distillation. When required it is also used to check the temperature of the fermenting mash. It is important that the thermometer is accurate at 78°C.

It must be a finely calibrated spirit thermometer, and can be graduated in whole degree divisions. Thermometers can be obtained ranging from 40°C to 90°C with 2/10ths degree accuracy. These are considerably more expensive. The right temperature is highly important. Partymanshop.com supplies thermometers that are all calibrated at 78°C.

Distillation Apparatus

The Still

A still of stainless steel is to be preferred, and will virtually last a lifetime. This type of still is quite expensive to buy, but use brings no deterioration in value. Stainless steel always looks new. A good still has a column. The column filling provides a good contact surface area, resistance that is not too high and good runback. A good stainless steel milking machine coupling is located between the column and the boiling vessel. The length of the column and the dimensions of the cooling tubes etc. are designed so that high steam resistance is avoided.

The apparatus is scientifically designed so that when the spirit is exhausted the process stops. No more spirit comes out of the cooler. There is a similar still with free drafts on the internet at www.moonshine-still.com. This still is highly recommended. It is as good as the Lab-Master, and instructions are great. Everything is free! Bob has done a marvellous job making this still and providing the information for free. In the same spirit, Gert Strand of Sweden supports his work with free web space and bandwidth, and this site has many visitors! So many that Bob had to take down his email address (he got thousands of emails and could not answer them all).

Another great still is The Amazing Still at amazingstill.com. It is a Swedish invention that works without a stove, without cooling water, and no boiling is involved. It is so simple that it really is amazing!

The Amazing Still produces very pure alcohol (35-45%), and is better than almost any stainless steel still. The process maintains itself. No oversight is necessary. The Amazing Still can be built in 15 minutes, and no welding is involved. Everything is free on the site, including a free eBook in many languages.

To improve The Amazing Still even more, a special yeast called **Prestige Turbo Pure**, has been developed. With this still, most users also collect the fore shots which can contain unwanted substances. Turbo Pure does not produce these substances and is therefore the only recommended yeast for The Amazing Still.

Lastly, there is **The Easy Still.** It is a 4 litre table top still with its own air cooling. It makes home distillation as easy as making coffee. You will find lots of great free info and instructions at easystill.com.

There are lots of copycat stills pretending to be The Easy Still. They are not the same – but they look identical. The Easy Still is a factory rebuilt water distiller. Some companies sell water distillers as alcohol distillers – these stills are very dangerous to use for alcohol distillation, as they can cause a big explosion.

This is because cooling works only for water, and cannot cool all alcohol to liquid phase. There are several problems with the imitation stills; most common is the "dancing lid".

Distillation column filling

A good column filling should be 3-6 mm in size, have a large surface area and be smooth in order to impart a fast and even runback.

Glass spheres (marbles) and the like are generally too large to give a good fractionation in the column. One can say that a column filling should be one tenth of the diameter of the column, but this is not absolutely correct. For example, with 5 mm glass spheres in a 50 mm wide column the vapour resistance will be too high. If the spheres are the right size, the surface area will be too small. The column filling is a once-only cost, so it must be correct from the start.

6 mm Raschig rings of porcelain are the best for 40 to 75 mm wide columns. They look like small pieces of cut tube and have an enormous surface area (both inside and out). The surface area is 940 against less than 300 for the corresponding spheres without holes through, and they are the best that is available.

Another column filling are called Saddles, which come in ceramic and metal. 4-5 mm size Saddle fillings work fine.

Raschig rings are used widely as boiling stones (for distributing heat in boiling vessel) both in the chemical industry and in boiling, for example, where it is desired to keep an even and exact boiling rate.

Raschig rings are available from specialist suppliers. 1 Litre of filling is sufficient for a normal column (600 mm high and 50 mm in diameter). As a stopgap one can use a metal net, brass, or stainless steel scrubs pads or 6 mm stainless steel nuts (expensive), etc. Do **not** use kitchen copper or stainless steel kitchen pads as column filling without the manufacturers guarantee that they are made from **food grade material**, in case they contain **lead** or dangerous metals.

Both the column and column filling must be cleaned thoroughly before each distillation, and must be cleaned after each distillation. A good cleaner is **Glasrens**, a winemaking cleaning agent used for cleaning of demijohns and bottles. To learn more about column fillings, visit www.raschig-rings.com.

Counter-flow rinsing of column

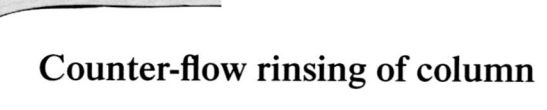

After the apparatus has been used the column should always be rinsed out with (preferably hot) water. One flushes water from the top through the distillation channel in the opposite direction through the entire column. This flushes out most of the impurities that have stuck in the column and column filling. Then it is a simple matter to remove the column filling for a thorough cleaning.

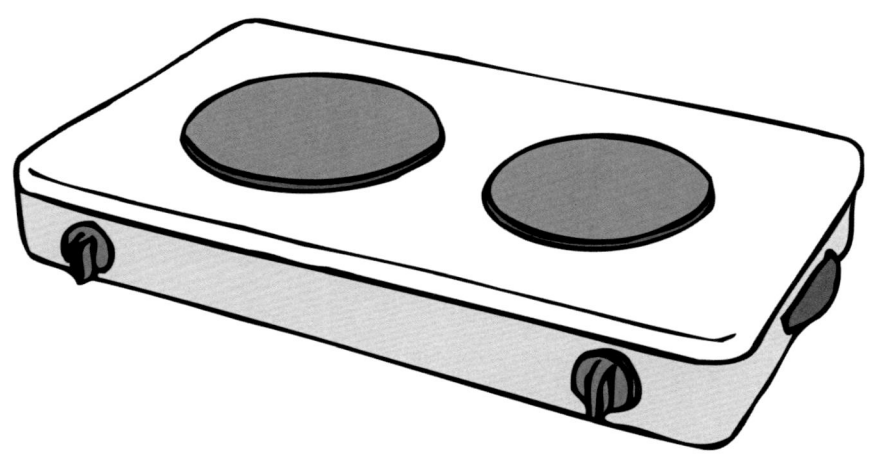

Heat source for the still

For a modern stainless steel still, both gas and electricity are suitable sources of heat, but electricity is safer to work with then an open flame. If the still has straight run-through cooling in the column the hotplate need not be infinitely variable. An ordinary boiling plate is suitable, but the best is a standard hotplate. These have a higher capacity. If the cooker has a cooker hood above it, hindering placing the still upon it just roll out the cooker from the wall (99% of domestic cookers are provided with castors).

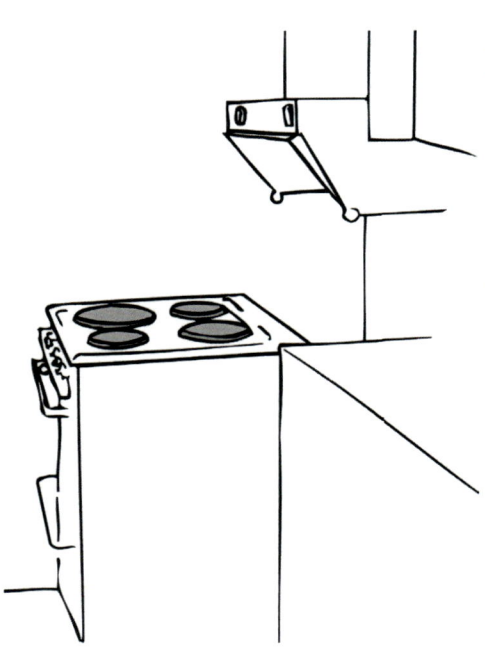

NOTE: Hotplates with a thermostat are unsuitable as the temperature is too variable, and also the mash vessel will surge boil.

An integral heating element is an excellent solution, but one must ensure that the mash vessel does not boil dry. If the element is not covered with liquid it will melt. A heating element heats the mash up faster and uses less electricity.

For determining temperatures for various purposes and also for reading the column top temperature one usually uses a laboratory thermometer graduated from -10 to 100°C or there about.

A thermometer can give a false reading so test it in boiling water, which should read +100°C at sea level (details at page 62. You can also use the on-line boiling point calculator at partyman.se/calculator.html. If the thermometer is not correct it will also read incorrectly at 78°C. Just make allowances for the error.

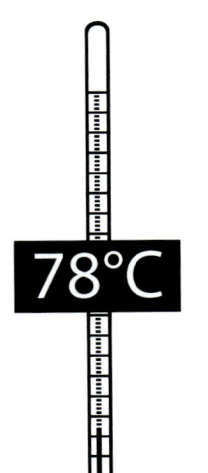

The Thermometer

The most important task for the thermometer is to determine the temperature at the top of the column during distillation. It is important that it is accurate (calibrated) at 78°C. Graduation in whole degrees is sufficient.

Page 23

Electronic Temperature Control

The distillation apparatus functions satisfactorily without such equipment. Using equipment for automatic temperature control frees one from personally monitoring the temperature. Many types of such controls are available. A transducer is mounted in the top of the column set at 78°C. It then controls the heating or the through cooling (using solenoid valves) if the temperature becomes too high.

Normally on the Lab-Master, no electronic temperature control is necessary. Of course it can sometimes be fun and need not cost a lot. The first solution is to put a thermostat in the top of the column. The thermostat then switches off the heating current if the temperature becomes too high. In practice this is not a good solution as the system is slow to respond as the thermostat requires a few degrees before responding. Distillation ceases as the heat source takes some time to heat up again on being once more switched on. Distillation will be 50% slower. The only use for such a system is as a "safety valve". If the temperature is set a few degrees too high, or if the temperature rises for any reason the thermostat will stop the distillation.

There are two reliable solutions that function well

1. A thermostat is placed in the top of the column. When the temperature becomes too high the thermostat switches off THE LAST element of the heat source. The distillation continues with a little less heat applied and does not stop in the "slow period". Then the thermostat switches on the current again, an inexpensive and effective solution.

2. An electronic temperature transducer is fitted in the top of the column. Note that this is a low voltage component and must be connected electronically.

When the temperature becomes too high the control redirects the current to the heat source via a rheostat (stepless power control) which is set to give slightly lower power to the heat source. This does the same thing as solution 1 but more accurately. An electronic temperature transducer is sensitive to one tenth of a degree, whereas a thermostat is accurate to 1-2 degrees. The electronic control can also be connected to a solenoid valve that opens an extra through-cooling in the column.

The LAB MASTER distilling apparatus

Column height 590 mm

Length of cooler 200 mm

Distance between first and second through-column 50 mm

Distance between the milking machine connector and the first through-column cooling tube 60 mm

Comments: The length of cooler is only 200 mm because the manufacturer will not make it longer. This is to prevent too rapid distillation with consequent bad results (one soon reduces distillation speed if warm spirit starts to run). The cooler can be made 50 to 100 mm longer but this is not vital.

The boiling vessel

The boiling vessel is fabricated from two stainless steel buckets (or saucepans or kitchen pots) welded rim-to-rim of 10-15 Litres capacity each. The capacity of the boiling vessel is 20-30 Litres. If the base buckles outwards, when stood on a hotplate, hammer it carefully slightly concave with a mallet or similar. If two stainless steel bread pans are used instead the boiling vessel will be lower and wider. This is almost better as heating up will be quicker. The boiling surface (vapour area) is bigger and distillation is more rapid.

These are the two most used types of boiling vessels. By using bread pans or buckets which are manufactured as standard products one saves much money. Custom or special purpose fabricated vessels in stainless steel are quite expensive.

The boiling vessel can be designed differently to give a faster distillation (wide vessel with a broad column junction), but the increase in speed compared with a bucket or dough trough vessel is of no consequence.

Material

Austenitic stainless steel or copper

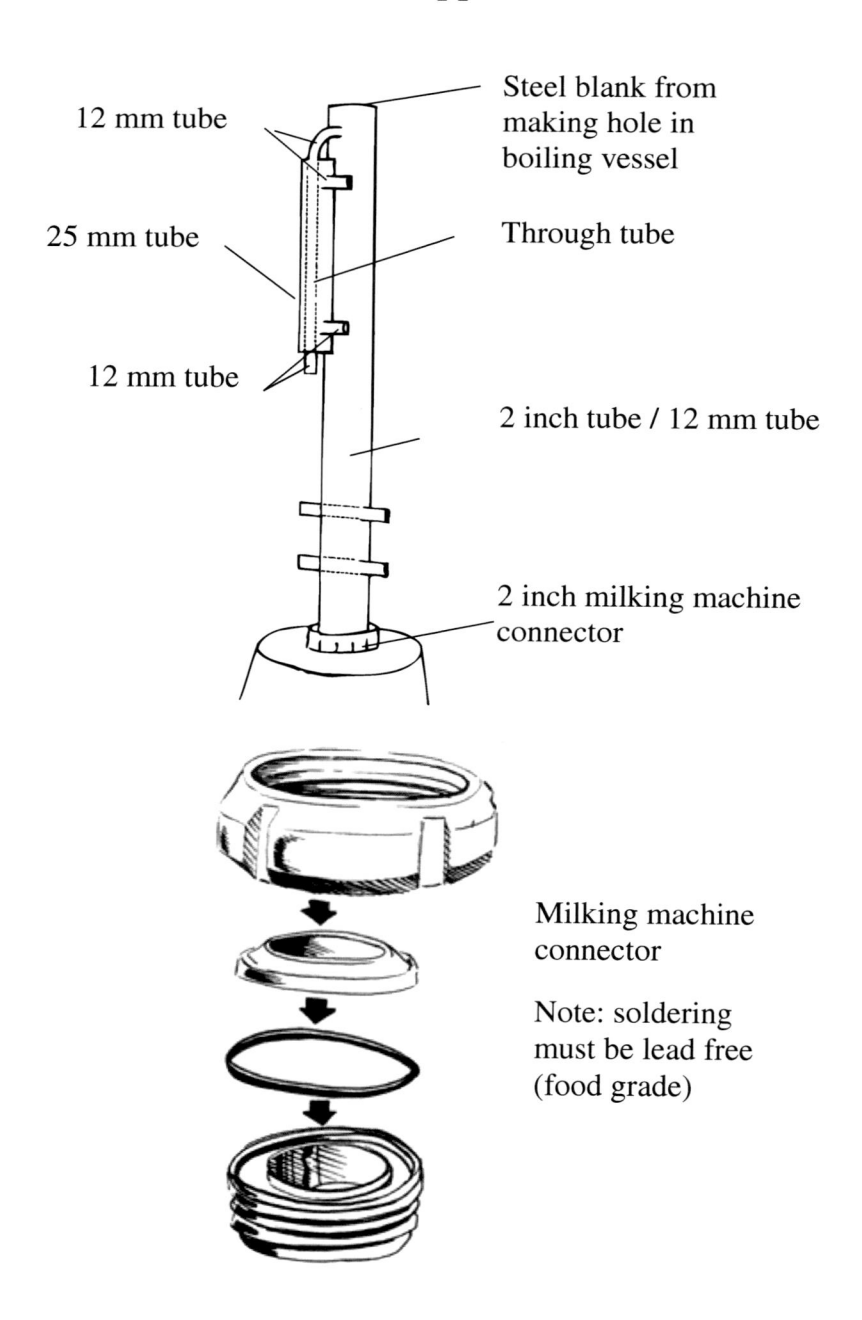

12 mm tube

25 mm tube

12 mm tube

Steel blank from making hole in boiling vessel

Through tube

2 inch tube / 12 mm tube

2 inch milking machine connector

Milking machine connector

Note: soldering must be lead free (food grade)

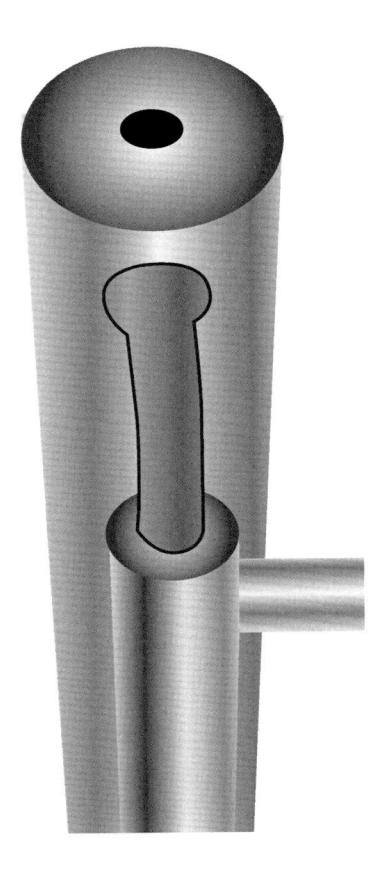

Thermometer connection point

The connection point is a 12 mm hole drilled in the top. In this a rubber grommet for the thermometer is placed. The same type as used in electrical equipment. An ordinary laboratory thermometer is inserted in the grommet.

As viewed from base of column

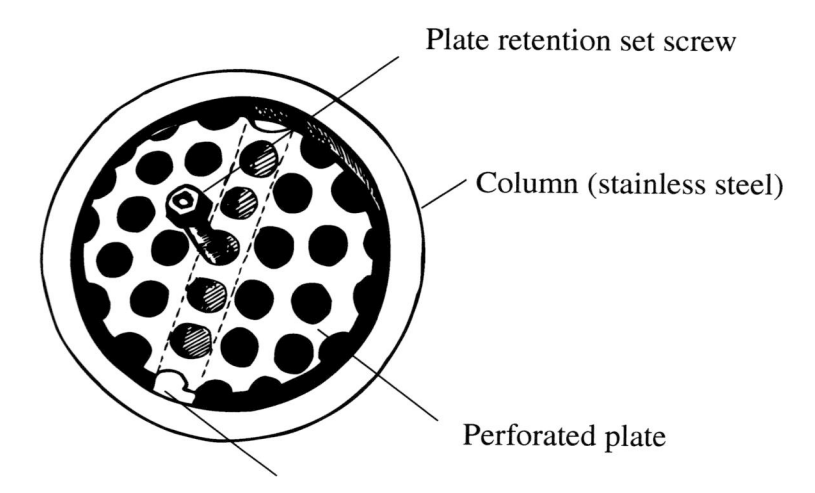

Plate retention set screw

Column (stainless steel)

Perforated plate

Strip welded at both ends mounted across column

Mounting of column filling Retention strip

A small strip of stainless steel is welded across the column, with fixing for a 5 mm stainless steel set screw. The plate for the retention of the column filling is provided with a centre hole as well as a number of other holes for the passage of the vapour.

Place the plate with centre hole onto the set screw and retain with a stainless steel nut. The plate can subsequently be easily removed when the column filling is to be removed or filled.

Fixing of column filling retention plate

A small stainless strip is welded across the base of the column, onto which is welded a small stainless steel set screw. The perforated plate is then attached to this.

The perforated plate is provided with a centre hole which receives the set screw and a stainless steel nut holds the perforated plate, which in its turn retains the column filling.

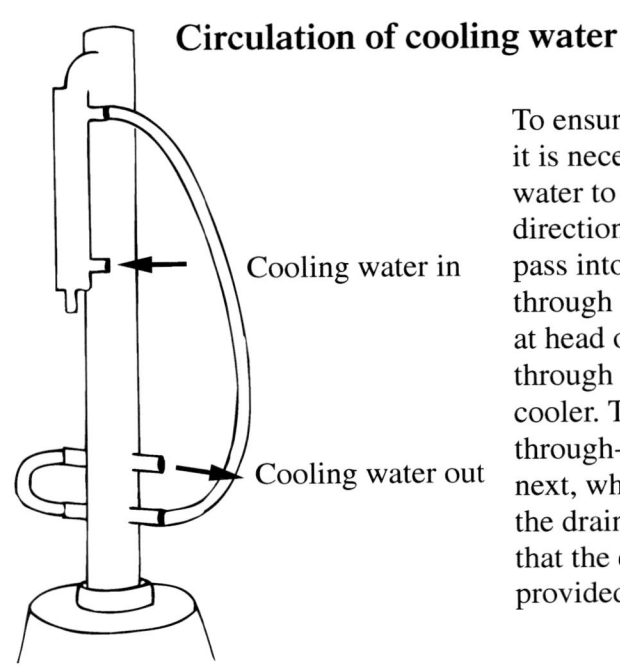

Circulation of cooling water

Cooling water in

Cooling water out

To ensure perfect distillation it is necessary for the cooling water to circulate in the correct direction. The cooling water is to pass into the base of the cooler, through the discharge point at head of the cooler and then through to the lower through-cooler. Then on to the next upper through-cooler (and then to the next, where provided) and onto the drain. This sequence ensures that the coldest cooling water is provided in the correct sequence.

These pictures are examples of parts purchased for next to nothing from a metal recycler.

Ingredients

Quantities

The quantities given in this book are Metric, which is the system used in Scandinavia. Equivalents are as follows:

METRIC / USA / UNITED KINGDOM

1 Litre / 1.06 US quart / 0.88 quart
1 kg / 2.20 US pounds / 2.20 lbs.
1 hectogram / 3.50 oz / 3.50 oz
1 gram / 0.56 drams / 0.56 drams
12 mm / 0.468 inch / 0.468 inch
25 mm / 0.975 inch / 0.975 inch
51 mm / 1.989 inch / 1.989 inch
59 cm / 23.23 inches / 23.23 inches
12 mm / 1/2 inch / 1/2 inch
25 mm / 1 inch / 1 inch
51 mm / 2 inches / 2 inches
59 cm / 23 inches / 1.94 foot
1 cm = 0.39 inch / 1 inch = 2.54 cm / 1 inch = 2.54 cm
1° Centigrade / 33.8° Fahrenheit
20° Centigrade / 68° Fahrenheit
30° Centigrade / 86° Fahrenheit
78° Centigrade / 172.4° Fahrenheit

CONVERSION

Fahrenheit = °C x 9/5 + 32 (multiply by 9; divide by 5; add on 32; the answer is in Fahrenheit.

For all kind of conversations online:
distillery-yeast.com/distillery-tips/converters/

Water

We use ordinary tap water. The only requirement: it must be drinkable water.

Sugar

We use ordinary granulated sugar.

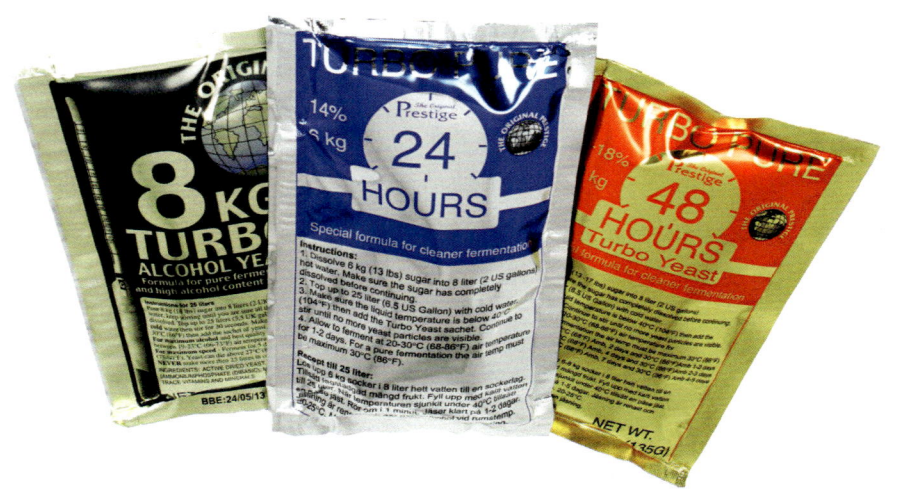

Yeast

It is best to use Turbo Yeast, the common name for a sachet with a mixture of nutrients and distillers yeast. There are two types. One produces 14% alcohol and one produces 18%. Under ideal conditions, one can produce 20% alcohol. Turbo Yeast has the ability to ferment pure sugar to alcohol, producing as few volatiles as possible. It is very hard to ferment only sugar and water to alcohol, but it is easy with Turbo Yeast. There are also a lot of low-quality Turbo Yeasts, thus a lot of volatiles are made. Use the Prestige Turbo Yeast to compare with other brands; use it if it is available at your supplier; or order it with affordable freight online: allfreightfree.com/homebrewing/turbo-yeast.html/

Prestige Turbo Pure is the purest fermenting yeast available. Prestige Black Label is the yeast used by commercial distilleries to produce up to 17% alcohol, but in consumer packing. Both are temperature tolerant. Prestige Black Label is also used for fuel alcohol. If one cannot get good Turbo Yeast, one uses ordinary baker's yeast: usually fresh packets (blocks) from a baker or yeast supplier. Dry yeast is just as good. It is not possible to produce high percentage alcohol with baker's yeast. It is better to aim for 11% alcohol, as it is possible to achieve.

Yeast Nutrients

In order to feed the yeast and to reduce the production of fusel oil we use yeast nutrients. The most important nutrient for yeast is nitrogen. Usually one adds 25-200 grams of macro nutrients (to supply nitrogen) for the fermentation of 25 Litres of mash. With rapid fermentation, however, Turbo Yeast gives a faster and much purer fermentation. Good Turbo Yeast is a mixture of macro and micro nutrients and distillers yeast. There are lots of low quality brands, Prestige is always great and can be used to compare other brands. This is simply because the producers pack the same yeast they supply distilleries with (at their industrial site distillery-yeast.com) in consumer packaging.

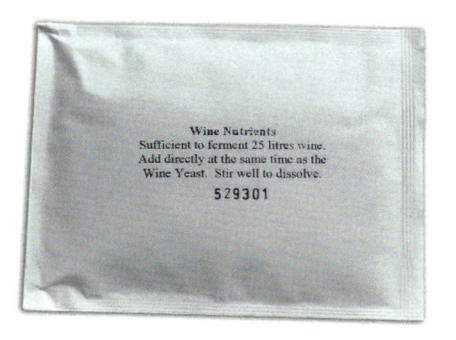

To ferment 14-15% one must use macro nutrients and yeast. Turbo Yeasts contain (expensive) micro nutrients, and can make 14% alcohol content easily. It is easier than those without macro nutrients.

To ferment over 15% you need the expensive micro nutrients, if you don't the fermentation will stop at a maximum of 14-15%.

On top, there are different regulations in different countries for the use of nitrogen nutrients. Because of this all Turbo Yeast in Oceania (Australia and New Zealand) have more than double the weight – and are not as good – as those for the rest of the world.

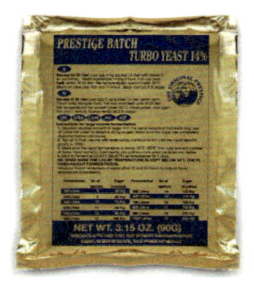

Turbo Yeast

To achieve a faster fermentation, Turbo Yeast is used. It is available in a number of brands, e.g., Prestige Black Label and Prestige Batch. Fermentation will be completed in 2-3 days, depending on how much sugar is used and the temperature, giving an alcohol content of 14-17%.

To obtain a stronger mash, Prestige Turbo Pure 18% is one of the best. It does what is claimed of it and gives a mash containing 18% alcohol, in optimum cases (using glucose as sugar) +20%. This means more spirits from the apparatus with the same quantity of mash. Prestige Turbo Pure is the purest fermenting yeast available and improves all home distillation.

If you live in a warm country, I would recommend Prestige Black Label and Prestige Turbo Pure because of their outstanding temperature tolerance. There is a lot of free info at www.turbo-yeast.com and info for distilleries and fuel alcohol distillers at www.distillery-yeast.com.

The best Turbo Yeasts come from Sweden and are made by Gert Strand AB. For price and quality, Black Bull Turbo from Denmark, is good. In the Oceania region, Prestige Oceania Turbo is the best.

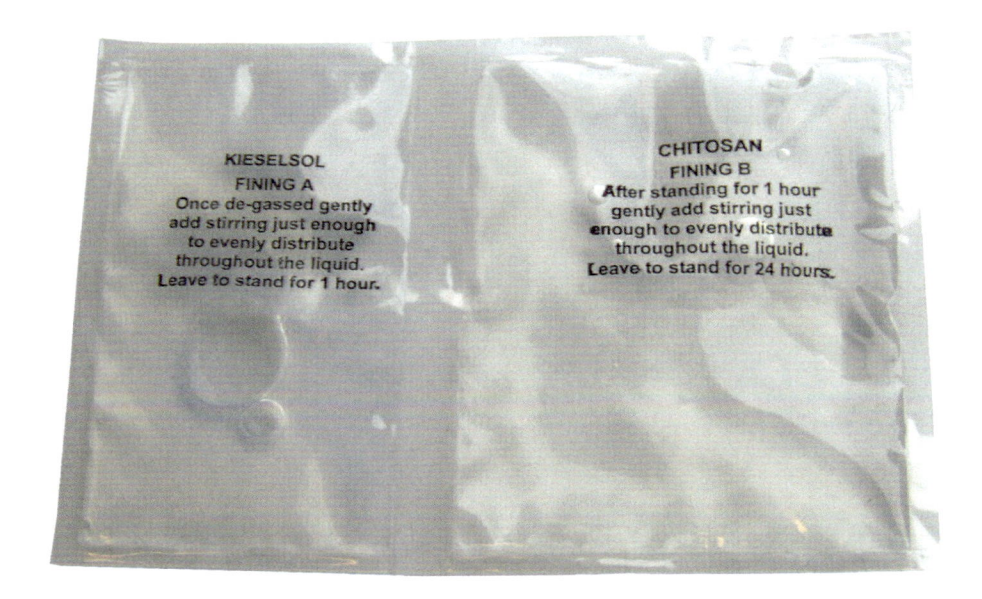

Clearing Agents (Finings)

When the mash has fully fermented it must clear. The mash will clear itself over time (it is just a question of waiting). To speed this process up a clearing agent (preferably chitosan based) can be used. It is the same type of clearing agent used for wine.

The mash is transferred to another fermentation vessel, leaving the yeast deposit. A clearing agent is added. Clearing can be speeded by cooling, placing the mash in a cool or cold location. After clearing, the mash is transferred over to the distilling apparatus with a siphon. The bottom deposits (lees) are then discarded.

Activated Carbon

Activated carbon is available in hundreds of different forms that are characterised by their absorption structure and special porous makeup. The carbon gets its characteristics from the method of manufacture and the basic raw material. The carbon absorbs impurities by virtue of many different effects. The carbon is very porous with a large surface area, usually 400-1600 square metres per gram. The pores can be described as an enormous number of naturally occurring cracks or pores that have randomly fused together into a coherent structure. Carbon can be compared to small sponges where impurities fasten in the holes. Absorption comprises an interaction of the exterior and interior surfaces that powers the active strength. Carbon has chemical, physical and electrostatic attributes.

Activated carbon can be made from crushed coal or made from various materials such as wood, coconut husk, peat or by-products of the oil industry. Ordinary coal is not active and contains many substances such as tar, etc. When coal is used as a fuel these substances give off heat. When activated carbon is made ordinary carbon is heated to a very high temperature of over 1000°C. The various substances are driven off as gas and leave the carbon. The process also charges the carbon electrically.

What remains is a sponge like porosity. Certain substances in various raw materials are driven off at different temperatures, and using this effect the porosity can be controlled. In order to make further pores, steam at 130°C is injected into the 1000°C hot carbon.

By selecting the raw material, temperature and form of treatment (steam, hydrogen super peroxide, etc.,) the appearance of the pores, the number of pores, (measured in square metres per gram, usually being between 400 and 1600) and the size and distribution of the macropores, mesopores, and micropores, can be tailor made.

Raw materials differ in weight, thus coal, for example, weighs twice as much as peat, which for the same volume gives it double the price for the carbon. Certain materials contain a large amount of substances that are removed by steaming, thus giving a big absorption area. These pores are tailor made for the purpose (they are formed and sized so that fusel oil, etc. fit exactly in the pores). In consequence there are only a very small number of suitable forms of activated carbon for purifying alcohol.

Apart from the pores sized so that the relevant impurities are trapped in them, the activated carbon is also electrically charged. Impurities fasten onto the surface of the carbon as though magnetically attracted. When filtering through a tube do **not** filter through twice, as the second time the impurities attracted to the outside of the particles will be removed. Apart from the structure of the carbon, three other factors are significant: **particle size, contact time and contact area.**

The most important thing, when using granulated activated carbon for alcohol purification, is **that it must be pre wetted.** Then the alcohol will pass **through** the carbon granules. Otherwise the purification will only take place on the surface of the activated carbon granules.

A complete E-book about activated carbon can be downloaded for free at books24-7.com/activated-carbon.html.

Activated carbon is always active

Activated carbon is electrically charged (can be compared to a magnet) and always remains active. However, it can happen that the carbon can be saturated with impurities. When saturated there is no room to absorb the impurities, both in the pores and on the surface.

If the impurities are removed the carbon will function again. Regeneration requires a lot more work than buying fresh activated carbon, so using new activated carbon is common and regeneration is seldom done at home.

The method for regeneration of activated carbon at home is with steam. When steam from 3 Litres of water (this takes hours) from a steam cleaner has passed through 1,7 Litres of activated carbon, it cleans properly. It is not recommended for savings, since the work is not worth it.

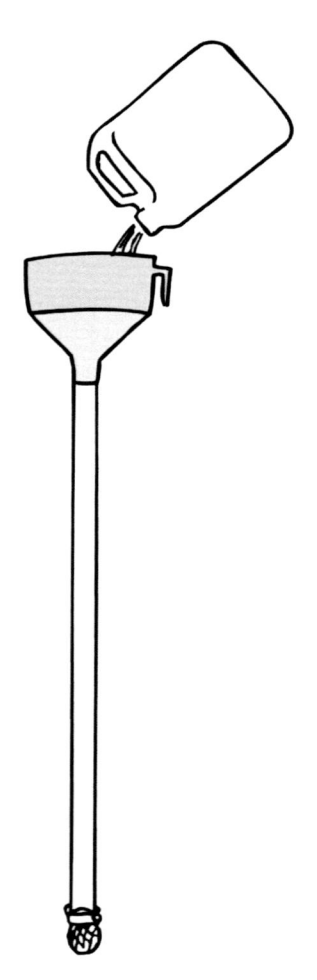

How much activated carbon is used?

Most types of carbon have the same characteristics, 1.7 Litres is sufficient for 4-5 Litres of 40-45% spirit. Some brands can purify double this amount. THE BEST purifying method is to use a long tube and filter through a wet carbon layer. Sometimes purification is not perfect. Filtering again with new carbon will give brilliant results. The new carbon will retain most of its absorption ability and can be used as the first filter for the next distillation. This method costs only one portion of carbon.

On the other hand – especially when activated carbon is perfectly wet – it can happen that less carbon is needed. It is just to taste and smell the alcohol.

Aquarium charcoal

Note that aquarium charcoal cannot be used with satisfactory results. It is manufactured from the most varied of raw materials, such as animal bones, blood, sphagnum moss, etc. Its purifying efficiency is very poor and the grain size is unacceptably coarse. The use of cheap raw materials means that the charcoal sometimes imparts off-flavours, and can even leave the alcohol tasting worse than if it had been unfiltered.

Deposits in the spirit

Sometimes a deposit is seen in the spirit. Usually this is calcium and minerals from the water used for dilution. Soft, distilled or mineral free water should always be used for dilution.

Certain type of activated carbon can give a grey carbon deposit in the spirit. Sometimes this can be cured by re-cycling the first half Litre. It is also important to use a good quality filter paper. With the pre wetting method for filtration one first washes the carbon from the soap-like substances that can make deposits. Then there cannot be any deposits from the carbon.

Essences

Briefly about the background to essences: In the commercial spirits industry many products are flavoured with essences. This is very common but little known by the general public. Such essences are of high quality and impart a good flavour (whisky and brandy are improved by the addition of 10% of the real thing).

Essences have been developed almost to perfection. As a consequence, even the essences intended for home use have been improved, as they are a consumer version of the commercial ones. Many people buy Vodka and an essence and blend a good drink more cheaply, especially in Scandinavia. Essences are manufactured from various raw materials, often working with oils, concentrates, extracts or solutions of the original substances. These can be, for example: brandy oil, coffee oil, orange oil, caraway oil, dill oil, oil of aniseed or natural fusel oils.

Also with these are herbs, oak and spices. Sometimes these extracts are distilled so that they are stronger and purer. There are also aromatics made by analysing natural aromas and then manufacturing identical substances. There are also synthetic aromatics, but these are used less and less.

The technology is advancing at a very rapid pace, giving products of a quality one could only dream of just five years ago. A new technique, carbon dioxide distillation, is the process behind many of these advances. If we take a rum essence, this can, for example, comprise one or several base aromatics that are rum flavoured. Each of these aromatics can be made from a large number of ingredients. The rum flavour can then be tweaked with oils, vanilla, oak extract, spice extract and maybe a little glycerine and cane sugar molasses. On top of this, sometimes concentrated rum, if possible, will be added.

Burnt sugar (caramel colour E150) is used both for colour and for fullness and taste. The process can take a long time, sometimes many years to develop a good essence. Often hundreds of samples are used. Gert Strand in Sweden is the leader in essences, which are sold under the brand name Prestige essences. Refer to the Internet at www.partyman.se.

Essences are compositions of several flavours, oils, extracts, colours etc. Smaller liquor industries often use essences to compare with superior quality.

This is common for **liqueurs and Absinthe** and the reason that **small producers** often have **higher quality** then the big brands. On the other hand, the big brands selling millions of bottles do what they can to reduce the cost, accepting the quality to lower as long the sales is not affected.

This is the reason that one can make a liqueur at home using essences that often taste **better** then world leading brands (the same for numerous liquors but not for Scotch whisky and French Cognac).

Absinthe essences (from Prestige) **outperform** commercial Absinthe. This is because when making Absinthe one mix herbs and alcohol, soak it until taste have moved over to the alcohol. Then distil this mixture (similar to making Gin). During this boiling, that take hours, some of the finest aromas is hurt by the temperature during boiling.

Prestige Absinthe essence is made the opposite way. The same herbs are used but as extracts or oils. Each ingredient is of the best quality available. But the most difference is that each ingredient is made by itself. No boiling for hours, some are even made with the gentle carbon dioxide distillation. Some ingredients are made by a patented process only used by the supplier – that on top grows the best herbs and they do not sell them to others.

This produces an Absinthe far better than the distilled, simply because the flavours taste better. A quality they could not dream of when Absinthe was originally invented.

On top of this **most commercial Absinthes are not real Absinthes.** They lack the 35 mgs of thujone because there is no wormwood used. If the Absinthe **does not** smell of wormwood, then it **is not** real. That is the fact with many, if not most, large brands.

The reason for this is that Absinthe that contained thujone was banned in USA – the world's largest market - for decades. So Absinthe producers took out wormwood and sold Absinthe **without** thujone – but **did not** tell their customers.

Then people in the States imported Absinthe privately from Europe. This passed custom and people believed that they had outsmarted the system. But what they really got was **fake Absinthe**, and it passed custom because the authorities were aware that **there was no thujone in the Absinthe.**

Today 10 mgs of thujone is allowed in Absinthe in USA. It is not real Absinthe but far better than before.

With Prestige Absinthe essences one can mix alcohol and essences and **make real Absinthe** with 35 mgs (there is even one with 55 mgs) of thujone and a perfect taste. There is a large assortment of Prestige Absinthe essences, Absinthe spoons and accessories at absinthekit.com.

The advantages of essences

All spirits stored in oak casks contain fusel oil. This is part of the aroma of brandy, whisky, dark rum, etc. Excess fusel oil intensifies a possible hangover. Spirits blended from essences contain little or no fusel oil, hence one is more likely to feel fine the next day, unless one has drunk far too much, at which point they will suffer from alcohol poisoning by upsetting their body chemistry. For making liqueur, essences are superior to using fresh fruit.

All liqueurs (except coconut, where the flavour is weakened naturally with storage) made with essences can be stored indefinitely. If fresh fruit is used shelf life is limited to 3-6 months. The taste can be better when using essences.

Essences are often made with natural raw materials selected for their fine flavour, suitable for making liqueur, and subsequently concentrated. Precise amounts of vanilla and other refined ingredients are also added. It is cheaper to have essences in stock at home than finished spirits, as essences can be stored for years without problem.

Which essences are best?

In the opinion of the author the Prestige essences, from Gert Strand AB in Sweden, are the best.

Prestige essences are also sold to micro distilleries and the liquor industry in bulk and mini bulk at distillery-yeast.com.

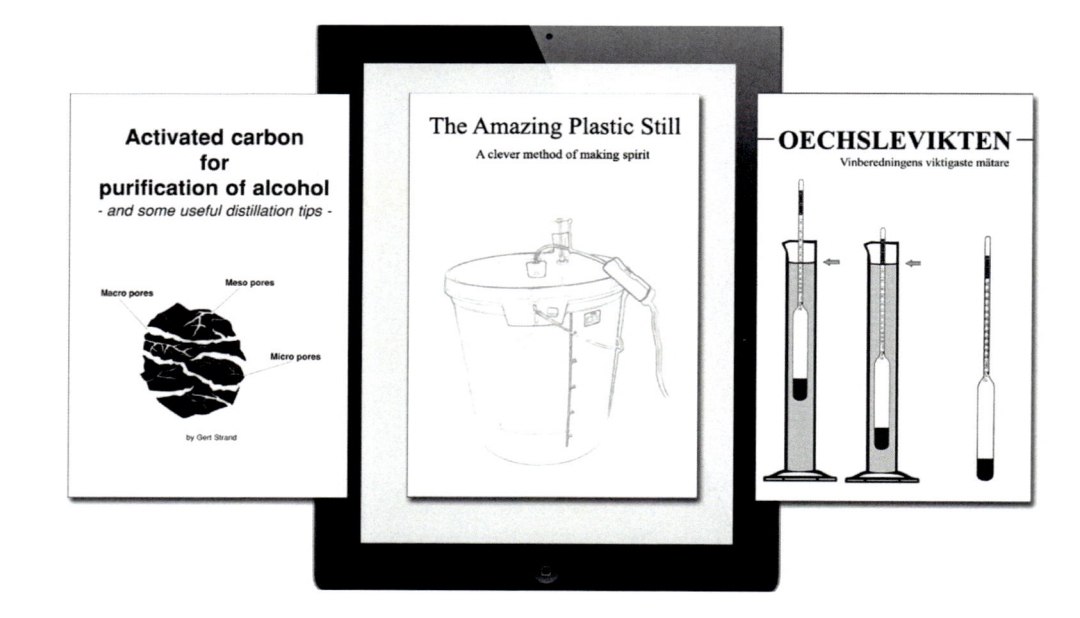

Literature about home distilling

Instructions on how to distill with The Easy Still – also how to use activated carbon purification on auto pilot during distillation – is on the website: www.easystill.com/how-to-make-spirits-at-home. Use Prestige Mini Turbo Yeast if you want to ferment 8 litre batches for The Easy Still.

For distillation of fruit brandy, grappa, etc. the author recommends the book: Handbuch für Schnapsbrenner (in German) by Dr. Helfried Schmickl at www.schnaps.co.at and the free book Artisan Distilling - A Guide for Small Distilleries by Professor Berglund at http://books24-7.com/artisan-distilling-a-guide-for-small-distilleries.html.

There is one great way to improve home-distilled whiskey: simply use real whiskey yeast with AG. It is available worldwide on the web at: www.whiskeyyeast.com.

Where to buy essences:

Sources

There are many places one can buy essences and accessories. The most usual are the internet, mail order, specialist shops, hardware stores, and department stores.

Look on the net for:

allfreightfree.com

partymanshop.com

For micro distilleries, distilleries, and absinthe manufacturers the best site is:

distillery-yeast.com

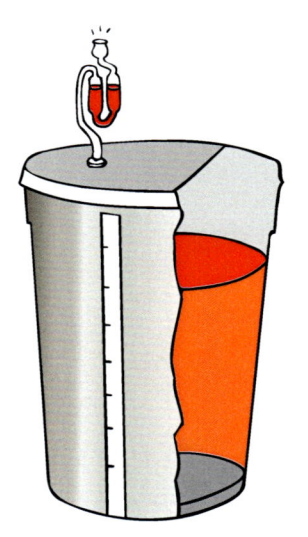

Mash fermentation

Preparing the mash

In principle, mash is cheap wine with no demands concerning taste. Only the alcohol is required, but the mash must contain as few impurities as possible, in order to give good results. Later the alcohol is separated by distillation. The simplest mash is comprised of sugar, baker's yeast, yeast nutrient salts, and water. The yeast consumes the sugar and produces carbon dioxide and alcohol.

The carbon dioxide bubbles out through the fermentation lock and the alcohol remains in the mash. But the yeast cannot "consume" endless quantities of sugar. If the concentration of sugar or alcohol is too high the yeast cannot work.

Ordinary baker's yeast, which we use, can ferment the mash up to between 11-13%, and then fermentation stops. Baker's yeast cannot work in a higher concentration of alcohol. To add more sugar than can be converted by the yeast is nothing but wasteful. For higher alcohol, Turbo Yeast must be used.

Mark the quantity of mash to be fermented on the outside of the fermentation vessel. Allow headroom of 20 cm, otherwise the mash will foam over.

So that all the sugar is fermented to alcohol the sugar must be completely dissolved in the water. 17 grams of sugar gives 1% alcohol in one Litre of mash. A 200 mm space should be left above the mash to allow for foaming. A 25 Litre container cannot ferment 25 Litres, but nearer 20-22 Litres.

During fermentation the yeast consumes the sugar, leaving two by-products, alcohol and carbon dioxide. The carbon dioxide "plops" out through the fermentation lock and the alcohol remains in the mash. So that the yeast is able to last as long as possible, it must be given optimal conditions. It is then given the best possible nutrition in the form of a yeast nutrient salt and an air temperature of between 20 and 25°C.

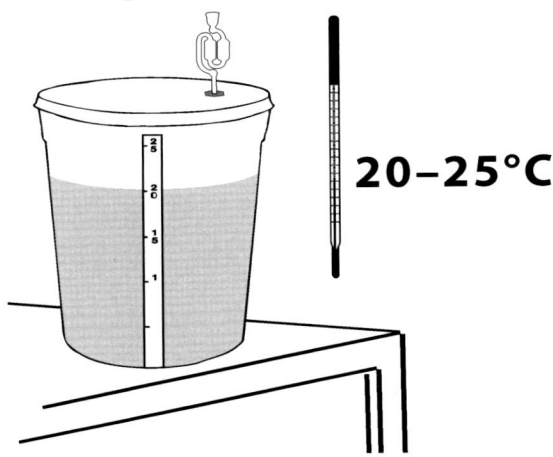

20–25°C

The fermentation process adds heat of about 5°C. If the liquid temperature falls below 18°C fermentation will stop until the temperature rises once more. A large surface area for the fermentation helps the carbon dioxide to leave the mash (so don't fill demijohns up to the neck).

Fermentation can be speeded by shaking the mash to get rid of the carbon dioxide, but do not shake rapidly fermenting yeast or the mash will leave the container. At 11-13% alcohol, the yeast rests and sinks to the bottom (at 14-18% with Turbo Yeast). This can be speeded up by using a wine clearing agent.

The clear mash is then transferred to the distillation apparatus and is distilled. Cleared mash must not stand on its lees for more than 3 weeks. It should be removed from the lees before the lees cause souring or oxidization.

When a mash does not ferment violently a fermentation lock filled with water must be fitted. The fermentation lock prevents air from coming into contact with the mash. If this happens the oxygen in the air and acetobacter can convert the alcohol to acetic acid. During fermentation the carbon dioxide, which is heavier than air, protects the mash like a protective cover. This is again a reason to leave 200 mm of space between the cover and the surface of the mash.

How much sugar is required?

Baker's yeast only manages to ferment up to 11-13% alcohol. 17 grams of sugar gives 1% alcohol in 1 Litre of mash. More sugar cannot be fermented out, so it is unnecessary to add more.

>221 grams per Litre of mash is used (13 x 17 grams).

>20 Litres of mash needs 4.5 kg sugar

>21 Litres of mash needs 4.7 kg sugar

>22 Litres of mask needs 4.9 kg sugar

>23 Litres of mash needs 5.1 kg sugar

>24 Litres of mash needs 5.3 kg sugar

>25 Litres of mash needs 5.5 kg sugar

>26 Litres of mash needs 5.8 kg sugar

>27 Litres of mash needs 6.0 kg sugar

>28 Litres of mash needs 6.2 kg sugar

>29 Litres of mash needs 6.4 kg sugar

>30 Litres of mash needs 6.6 kg sugar

Sugar can be measured with a Litre measure if you have no scales. 1.15 Litres of granulated sugar weigh 1 kg.

Special yeasts are available (Prestige Turbo Pure etc.) that can ferment up to 18% alcohol. Measure how many Litres are to be fermented, then calculate number of Litres x 18% alcohol x 17 grams sugar.

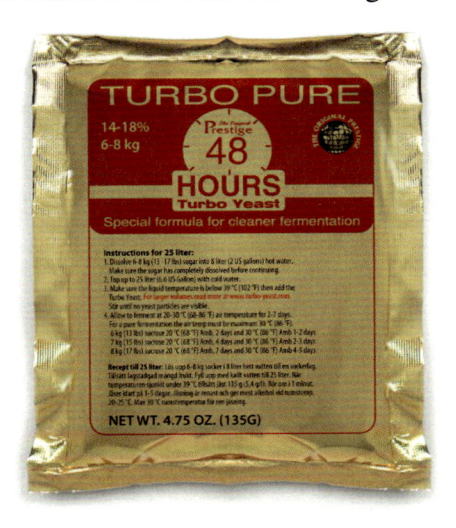

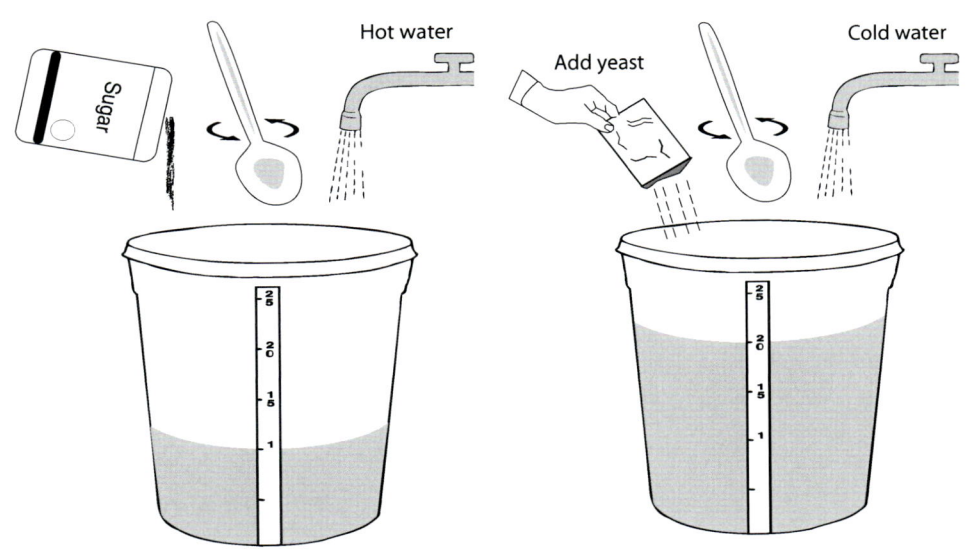

Example: 22 Litres of mash is to be fermented: 22 x18 x 17 = 6.732 g sugar or about 7 kg. Dissolve sugar in hot water until it is syrup, then fill up to 22 Litres with cold water and add the yeast.

Note that baker's yeast and ordinary Turbo Yeasts cannot ferment out more than 12-14% alcohol. Only high alcohol-tolerant yeasts can manage this, but take longer, 1-2 weeks and liquid temperature may not go over 30°C for 18% and 25°C for 20-21%.

Purer fermentation with Turbo Yeast

By using Turbo Yeast (the generic name) it is possible to ferment a mash with more alcohol and less volatiles in a short space of time.

Basically there are two types of Turbo Yeast, one that ferments 14% alcohol and one to ferment 18% alcohol. Then there are yeast strains that are temperature tolerant, and there are strains that are not.

Some strains can be used to make fruit schnapps and brandy because they extract the flavours from the fruit (Fruit Schnapps Yeast and Prestige Black Label) while others do not extract fruit flavours but make a very pure alcohol (Prestige Turbo Pure).

Turbo Yeast

Turbo Yeast is a mix of yeast, and complex macro/micro nutrients which will ferment a pure sugar solution into alcohol quickly. There are two types of Turbo, one making 14% of alcohol in three days, and one making 18% of alcohol in seven days.

The 18% Turbo yeast will get 50% more alcohol from the same distillation. The 14% Turbo Yeast will create a faster distillation, and 2 to 3% more alcohol than baker's yeast. Both types of Turbo give **less volatile residue** than with baker's yeast.

In Oceania all Turbo Yeast are **less** effective, and have to sold with double the weight of European Turbo Yeast because of ingredient regulations. Because of this the "killing temperature" gets lower, fermentation overheats, and the yeast dies at 13-15% alcohol. Most of the producers will claim 20% alcohol, but they do **not** say that this can only happen if glucose is used as sugar, and the temperature of the **liquid** fermentation is around 25°C.

Reality is that the room temperature is 25°C, or higher, and then the fermentation creates a lot more heat itself. This reaches the "killing temperature", and the fermentation stops, leaving a low alcohol content.

It is possible to improve fermentations by ordering yeast by mail order from outside Oceania, or by fermenting at a lower room temperature, 18-22°C (or by doing both). If you do import, Prestige Turbo Pure is the best.

The best turbo inside Oceania. But not as good as those in the rest of the world.

Some Turbo Yeasts and their characteristics

Black Bull Turbo is a temperature tolerant yeast that ferments to 17.5 – 18%, and extracts fruit flavours when used for brandy. At a low price and good quality Black Bull Turbo is probably the second best Turbo Yeast in the world.

Prestige Turbo Pure is a temperature tolerant yeast that ferments sucrose to 18% alcohol, and glucose to 20-21% alcohol.

It is the best yeast for The Amazing Still, (which uses vaporisation to produce extremely pure alcohol) as you don't have to separate the fore shots with this still.

Prestige Turbo Pure does not extract fruit flavours from fermentation; this yeast is for pure alcohol. It is also suitable for Alco Base (alcobase.com) that can be flavoured to RDT (Ready to drink) drinks.

Prestige 8 kg Turbo is not temperature tolerant, so you do not use it when the room temperature is high. It ferments 8 kg sugar to 18% alcohol. Extracts fruit flavours from fermentation extremely well.

Prestige Black Label ferments 6 kilograms of sugar to 14.5-15% alcohol. It can also ferment 7-8 kilograms of sugar. It is temperature tolerant, and extracts fruit flavours from fruit in fermentation. Prestige Black Label can also ferment Alco Base (alcobase.com) because of its very clean fermentation. It is also stackable, so you can ferment larger batches.

Turbo Extreme 23% is not temperature tolerant, and does not extract fruit flavours from fermentation. To ferment to 23% alcohol the yeast must have some "surface" to hang on to in fermentation. Many people use activated carbon powder to do this, but this will contaminate all equipment used. This Turbo uses other adsorbents.

In my opinion there is no need to use Turbo Extreme 23% because the 18-20% Turbo Yeast is cheaper, and their fermentation is very pure. Turbo Extreme 23% is only mentioned because there is no better 23% Turbo on the market today – and it is not so well known.

There are a lot of Turbo Yeasts on the market today, and I have listed these Turbo Yeasts as they are the best around. They mostly come from Gert Strand in Sweden – a small producer that always reaches the highest quality.

A note about whisky and fruit schnapps

Whisk(e)y is made by artisan distillation, and years of maturing. To make a good whisky one cannot use Turbo Yeast. One must use dedicated whisky yeast with AG, like Prestige WD Yeast (allfreightfree.com/homebrewing/yeast.html). Fruit schnapps and Fruit brandy gets a lot better with Fruit Schnapps Yeast.

This is a yeast strain similar to the one used in Prestige 8 kg Turbo, and uses micro and macro nutrients to reach 18% alcohol – but not to speed up fermentation.

What happens is fermentations are slow – several weeks. Because of this, close to no flavour will leave with the carbon dioxide (while most do in a fast Turbo Yeast fermentation). Almost all fruit flavours stay in the fermentation. Because fermentation reaches 18% a lot more flavour is extracted when fermenting to a lower alcohol level (add sugar to reach 18%).

I have tasted apple fruit schnapps from Dr. Schmickl's distilling school. They fermented their schnapps to 18% using this strain and the schnapps outperformed all the best commercial brands. Commercially in Austria you can't, by law, add more sugar to reach 18% alcohol in fermentation, to get more flavour from the apples. Dr. Schmickl's apple fruit schnapps tasted so good that I could taste what kinds of apples were used. This was a test and done by a master artisan distiller – but it was also the yeast strain that helped to make it possible.

Basic instructions:

1. Dissolve sugar (usually 6 kg) in warm water, and then fill up with cold water to give a volume of 25 Litres. The sugar must be completely dissolved to be able to ferment to alcohol.

2. Add the Turbo sachet contents and then leave somewhere warm for a few days, so the yeast can convert all the sugar into alcohol (fermentation). Using 6 kg of sugar you end up with a liquid (the "mash" or the "wash") of approx. 14% alcohol.

The clear mash is then drawn off and distilled to concentrate the alcohol to as near to 95% v.v. ethanol as possible and then treated with activated carbon to remove off-flavours and smell. More will be said about these instructions later.

What makes for a "good" Turbo?

It should be able to ferment to 14% alcohol in 3 days even when the temperature is not ideal (see later) equally important is that the mash produced contains only a small amount off-flavours or smell (the volatiles). The benefits of a rapid fermentation are obvious, but the importance of making a clean mash may not be so obvious since later treatment with activated carbon should remove these volatiles anyway. An explanation follows;

The key to making world-class spirits and liqueurs in the home

1. First make clean, pure ethanol.

2. Then use the best available essences to convert it.

A common mistake is to try to copy the traditional way spirits and liqueurs are commercially made. You will fail unless you use all the same raw materials, the same equipment, the same process control, and the same maturating processes. Get just one thing wrong and your result will be nothing like the commercial drink you are trying to match.

To illustrate what I am saying, look what happens when a Scotch whisky manufacturer changed just one detail of his traditional process;

This Scotch whisky maker decided to buy a new still. He went to great expense to ensure the new stainless steel still was exactly the same shape and size as his old copper one, knowing full well that any changes to shape or size would alter the character of his whisky.

The new still was installed and the virgin whisky (before maturation) was produced exactly as it had been before. The virgin whisky produced had an unpleasant turnip-like smell! The scientists could not explain why the move from copper to Stainless steel made such a difference, they put some copper back in the still to solve the problem! So unless you can copy everything down to the last detail, you will fail. In this case "Simple is best", use white granulated sugar, and a good Turbo!

Understanding the science of fermentation

You don't need to understand the science of fermentation to make good spirits and liqueurs in the home unless you want to experiment with the fermentation system i.e. fermenting larger volumes or higher alcohol levels. Seeing fermentation from the yeast's perspective helps in understanding the science. Yeast is a living organism actually very similar to the individual cells in our own body. It is easy to think of dried yeast as "just another ingredient" like the nutrients or the sugar but nothing could be further from the truth.

Yeast's sole aim in life is to reproduce; it does this by "budding" to produce a daughter cell identical to the parent. Given a plentiful supply of oxygen, sugar, minerals, enzymes, and amino acids, it will reproduce itself every 30 minutes. Then you will end up with a bucket full of yeast! Take away the oxygen and you will get much less growth, and a bucket full of alcohol. As far as the yeast is concerned sugar is a source of energy, the yeast cell imports (eats) a sugar molecule (e.g. Glucose) which has 6 carbon atoms joined together by chemical bonds. The yeast cell breaks these bonds one by one, each time releasing energy, which is used for growth. Without oxygen yeast cells can only break one bond, and so releases only a small amount of energy (so only a little growth). What's left is thrown out of the cell as a waste product, which is ethanol (alcohol). So, if you want to make alcohol, keep the oxygen out!

To grow, yeast also needs amino acids, enzymes, and minerals, as well as the energy it extracts from sugar. These are needed to build new proteins (by creating bonds between amino acids) and carry out the many enzymatic reactions within the cell. A good Turbo sachet will contain **all** of these essential growth ingredients collectively we call these "yeast nutrients". If you have ever tried to ferment pure sugar with just yeast, you will know that you get very little alcohol, which is because yeast needs these other nutrients as well as sugar.

Yeast is a living organism

So yeast is a living organism which uses sugar to make energy for growth. Without oxygen around yeast cannot extract all the energy from sugar, and throws out ethanol as a waste product. To function, yeast also needs amino acids, enzymes, and minerals which collectively we call nutrients. As well as throwing out ethanol as a waste product, yeast throws out another 1300 other compounds which we can call "volatiles".

These volatiles fall into chemical categories:
Higher alcohols (also called Fusel oils)
Esters
Carbonyl compounds
Organic acids
Sulphur compounds

All fermented alcoholic drinks contain these volatiles, whether made in the home or made commercially. It is basically the amounts and types of volatile that makes dark Rum taste and smell like dark rum, or, that makes whisky taste and smell like whisky.

It is important to make clean and pure ethanol when brewing at home. We **don't** want these volatiles. This is why activated carbon is used after distillation, to remove these volatiles. But, even the best activated carbons will not remove a large amount of volatiles, so it is important to try **not to** make them in the first place. Your choice of yeast strain, and nutrients have the greatest influence on keeping volatile production to a minimum.

The only control you have here is to buy **a good Turbo sachet**. It is the Turbo manufacturer's job to select the best yeast strains for the job, and use the correct nutrition. However, the temperature you use throughout fermentation and the activated carbon used all influence volatile concentration.

All about temperature

There are 3 types of temperature we need to talk about:

1: The air temperature

2: The liquid temperature

3: The killing temperature

Because yeast generates heat during fermentation, the liquid temperature will be higher than the air temperature. The difference between the two will increase as the volume you are fermenting increases. High temperatures will kill yeast. When there is no alcohol most yeast dies at 40°C, but as the alcohol increases the "killing temperature" decreases.

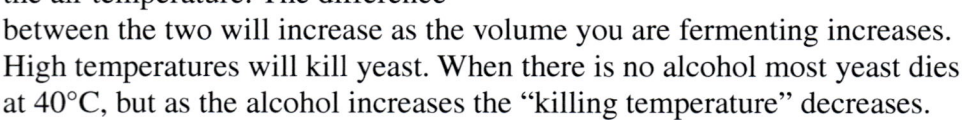

At 14% alcohol (which is what you get using 6 kg sugar in a 25 L volume) the killing temperature drops to 33°C (for Black Label Turbo it is 40°C) and at 20% alcohol down to 25°C.

If you use 17 grams of sugar, it will ferment to 1% of alcohol in 1 liter of mash. Providing you keep the liquid temperature below 30°C all the way through fermentation (25°C for very high alcohol) you will not kill the yeast. This is easy with volumes up to 25 Litres because the difference between air and liquid temperatures is only a few degrees.

But it is not so easy to keep the liquid temperature below 30°C when fermenting larger volumes. You either need to keep the heat generation down, or cool the liquid by introducing frozen 5 Litre water containers, after about 12 hours into the fermentation.

Prestige Batch and Black Label Turbo have been designed with this problem in mind. It is "fully stackable" up to 200 Litres, so use 1 sachet for 25 Litres, 2 sachets for 50 Litres, up till 8 sachets for 200 Litres.

Above 200 Litres you need to introduce cooling, or use fewer sachets (e.g. 16 sachets for 600 Litres). You now understand why it is important to keep the liquid temperature below 30°C. There is another reason to keep the liquid temperature below 30°C - to keep volatile production down to a minimum. In fact, the lower the fermenting liquid temperature, the lower the volatiles. So you could say "the cooler the better", however, in practice the amount of volatiles produced at a very cool temperature like 15°C is not much less than at say 25°C.

But there is a huge difference in fermentation time, at 25°C fermentation of 6kg / 25 Litres, will take 3 days, but at 15°C it will take nearly 2 weeks! To keep down production of volatiles a liquid temperature of 25°C is recommended.

Some different quality Turbos

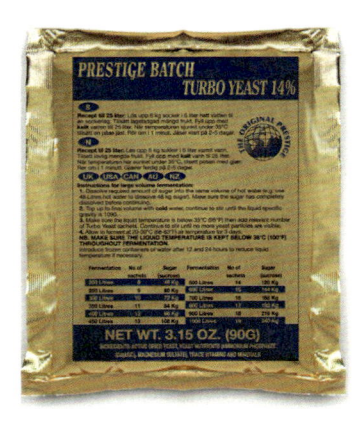

Black Label Yeast and Prestige Batch

To make 14.5% ethanol in 3 days, use
1 sachet + 6 kg sugar in 25 Litres, or use 8 sachets +
48 kg sugar in 200 Litres (or anything in between,
e.g. 5 sachets + 30 kg sugar in 125 Litres).

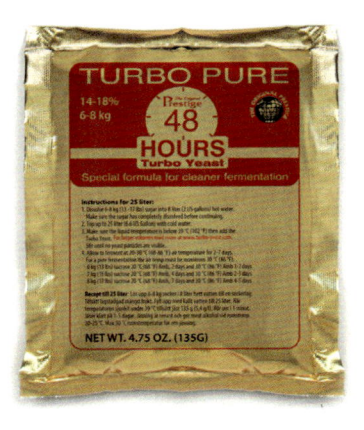

Prestige Turbo Pure 18%

To make 18% ethanol in 7 days, use 1 sachet + 8 kg sugar in 25 Litres. Use 10 kg glucose sugar to make 20-21% in 2-3 weeks. It is not recommended to scale up to larger volumes unless you have good control of liquid temperature.

Turbo Yeast instructions for 25 Litres

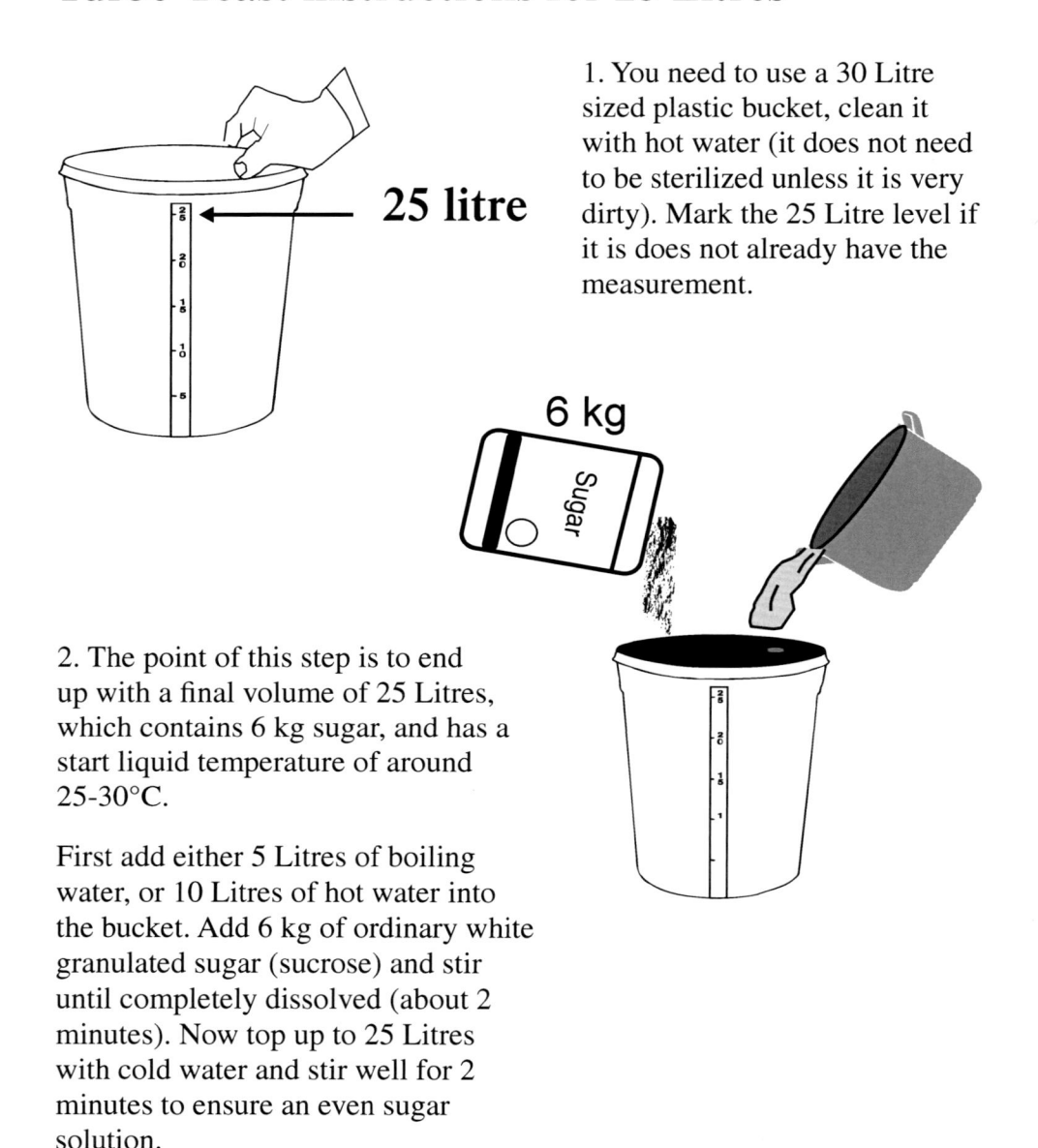

1. You need to use a 30 Litre sized plastic bucket, clean it with hot water (it does not need to be sterilized unless it is very dirty). Mark the 25 Litre level if it is does not already have the measurement.

2. The point of this step is to end up with a final volume of 25 Litres, which contains 6 kg sugar, and has a start liquid temperature of around 25-30°C.

First add either 5 Litres of boiling water, or 10 Litres of hot water into the bucket. Add 6 kg of ordinary white granulated sugar (sucrose) and stir until completely dissolved (about 2 minutes). Now top up to 25 Litres with cold water and stir well for 2 minutes to ensure an even sugar solution.

Ideally the cold water used for topping up should be between 15-20°C although water as low as 5°C can be used, this will just make the fermentation 1-2 days longer.

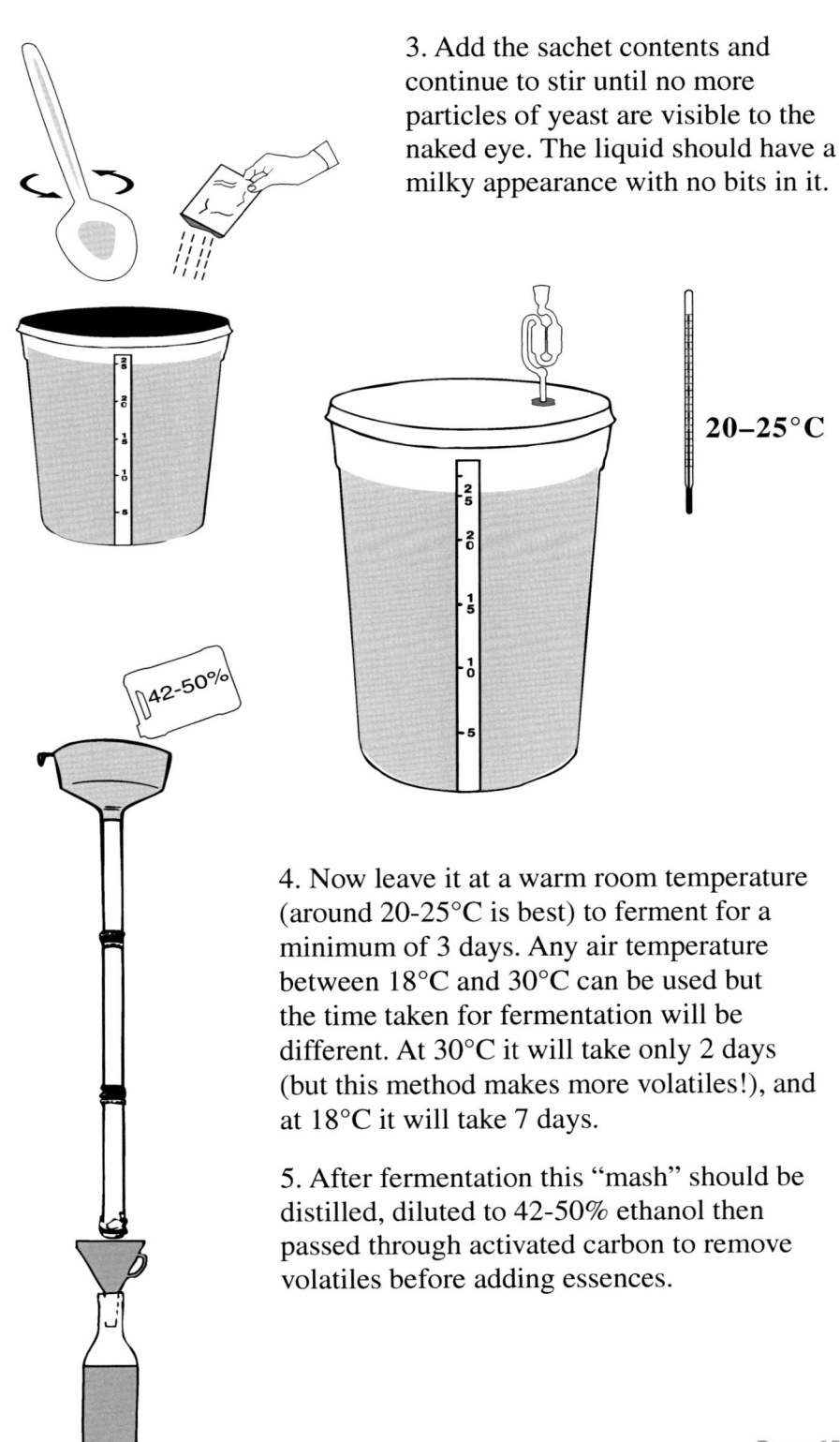

3. Add the sachet contents and continue to stir until no more particles of yeast are visible to the naked eye. The liquid should have a milky appearance with no bits in it.

20–25°C

42-50%

4. Now leave it at a warm room temperature (around 20-25°C is best) to ferment for a minimum of 3 days. Any air temperature between 18°C and 30°C can be used but the time taken for fermentation will be different. At 30°C it will take only 2 days (but this method makes more volatiles!), and at 18°C it will take 7 days.

5. After fermentation this "mash" should be distilled, diluted to 42-50% ethanol then passed through activated carbon to remove volatiles before adding essences.

Some words about quality

There are many Turbo manufacturers, and to make a good Turbo you need to have a lot of knowledge. For example, the content of a certain Turbo contains 22 different nutrients. Some producers only provide one nutrient, diammonium phosphate. Another example, some producer´s yeast ferments much faster when you use a mono sugar, like grape sugar (glucose). A good Turbo ferments sucrose (ordinary household sugar, dextrose) with the same speed up to 18% alcohol. All quality Turbo Yeast is designed to make as few volatiles as possible.

To manufacture good Turbo Yeast you need a great deal of knowhow. To make a bad Turbo (and there are many) you need only baker's yeast and diammonium phosphate. The first widely sold Turbo Yeast in Sweden, and probably the world, was Gert Strand's Superjasten.

Today Gert Strand has a huge range of high quality Turbo Yeasts, which are the same quality as he supplies to the distillery industry – but in consumer packaging. These are not hobby standard yeasts, this the same as a distillery use.

Turbo Yeast has become a generic name across the industry, and Gert Strand is one of the smaller producers. But, when it comes to quality, you won't find better.

A last trick to improve quality

When the mash has completely fermented (use a hydrometer to check), let it clear until it is crystal clear. Then draw off the mash with a siphon, leaving all yeast and impurities in the fermentation vessel. By this method you will have a crystal clear mash without yeast to distil. The mash should be able to clear by itself in a day or two. You can speed this up by adding a clearing agent for wine, or by placing the mash in a cool place. The mash must have fermented completely before clearing.

Large volume fermentation

1. Instructions to make more than 200 Litres using Prestige Batch or Prestige Black Label Turbo Yeast. The larger the volume the more difficult it gets to keep the liquid temperature below the lethal 37°C (for Black Label it is 40°C). The best number of sachets to use is as follows:

Fermentation Volume / No of sachets / Sugar (sucrose)

200 Litres / 8 / 48 kg

250 Litres / 9 / 60 kg

300 Litres / 10 / 72 kg

350 Litres / 11 / 84 kg

400 Litres / 12 / 96 kg

450 Litres / 13 / 108 kg

500 Litres / 14 / 120 kg

600 Litres / 15 / 144 kg

700 Litres / 16 / 168 kg

800 Litres / 17 / 192 kg

900 Litres / 18 / 216 kg

1000 Litres / 19 / 240 kg

Instructions for large volume fermentation

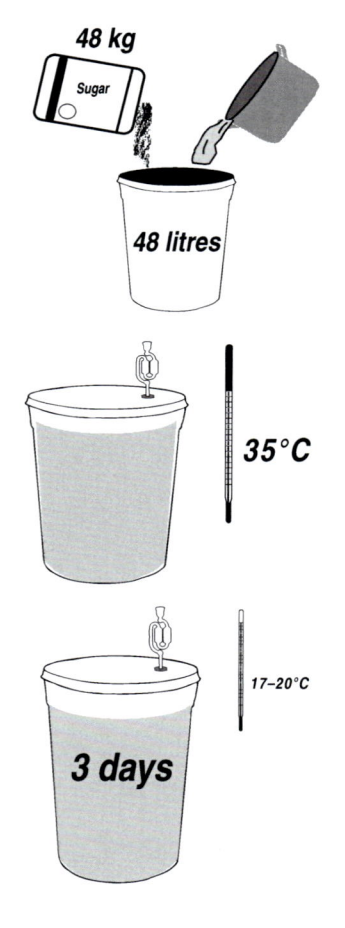

1. Dissolve required amount of sugar into the same volume of hot water (e.g. use 48 Litres of hot water to dissolve 48 kg of sugar). Make sure the sugar has completely dissolved before continuing.

2. Top up to final volume with cold water, continue to stir until the liquid specific gravity is 1090.

3. Make sure the liquid temperature is below 35°C then add relevant number of Prestige Batch sachets. Continue to stir until no more yeast particles are visible.

4. Allow to ferment at 17-20°C air temperature for minimum of 3 days.

NB. Make sure the liquid temperature is kept below 35°C throughout fermentation.

Introduce frozen CONTAINERS of water between 12 and 24 hours to reduce liquid temperature if necessary. One can also put a tube (plastic or copper) in the liquid and run cool water through the tube. I do not recommend the use of high alcohol Turbo Yeasts, after reflection, for any volume above 25 Litres. For larger volumes the liquid temperature must be tightly controlled between 24 - 26°C and this will not be possible in practice even by the most experienced people.

One can often find a way to ferment 18% in large batches by reducing fermentation speed, and thereby the heat production, by adding the sugar in 2 portions (2/3 + 1/3), or by reducing the amount of yeast to 2/3. One can learn about this at www.turbo-yeast.com.

Pot Distiller´s yeast.18%

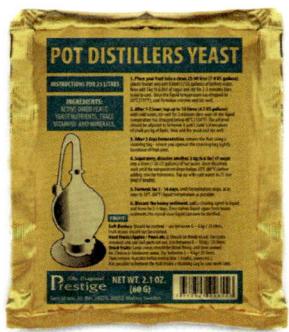

8 kg Turbo yeast 18%

Black Label 14%

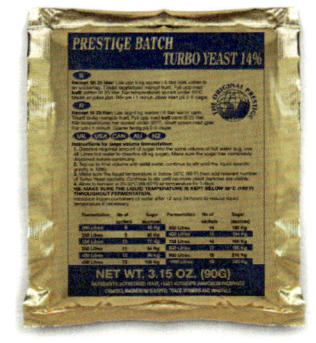

Prestige Batch 14%

Turbo Pure 14%

Turbo Pure 18%

There is also Fruit Schnapps Yeast and Pot Distillers Yeast for grappa, fruit brandy, etc. But do not use them for whisky. Whisky is made from beer, which needs a maximum 0.1 - 0.2 grams of nutrients per Litre mash. These Turbo have far too many nutrients for whisky, but are great for fruit brandy. Use Whisky Yeast with AG for whisky, and never make stronger mash then 8.5% if you do not use this whisky yeast. More info at: whiskeyyeast.com.

Mash fermentation with Turbo Yeast

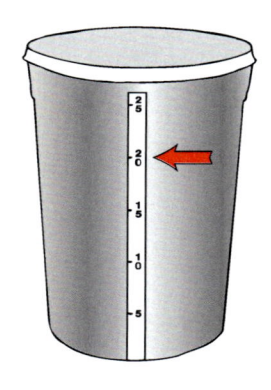

1. MARK OUT THE VOLUME

Make a level mark on the fermentation vessel, indicating how many Litres are to be fermented. Remember to leave at least 200 mm for foaming.

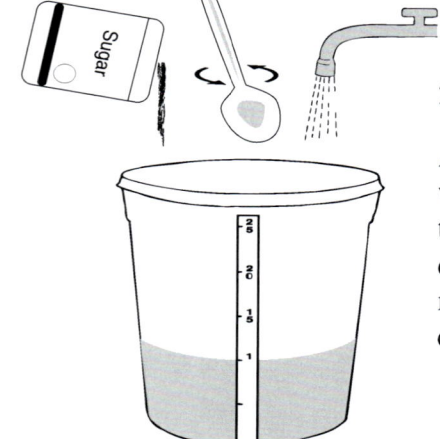

2. MIXING

Add 10 Litres of hot water from the hot water tap to the fermentation vessel. Add the sugar. Shake or stir until the sugar is completely dissolved. **NOTE:** the sugar must be completely dissolved before it can be fermented to alcohol.

3. ADD YEAST

Fill up the fermenting vessel with cold water. Fill up to the level marking. Add the Turbo Yeast and shake or stir vigorously. Fermentation will start in a few hours. Put the cover on without using the fermentation lock.

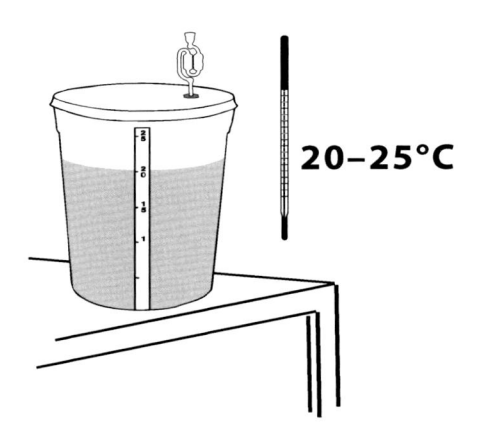

4. FERMENTATION

Fit the fermentation lock, with water in it, after 2 days fermentation, and press tight the cover. If water escapes from the fermentation lock, because of the speed of the fermentation, wait one day before refilling.

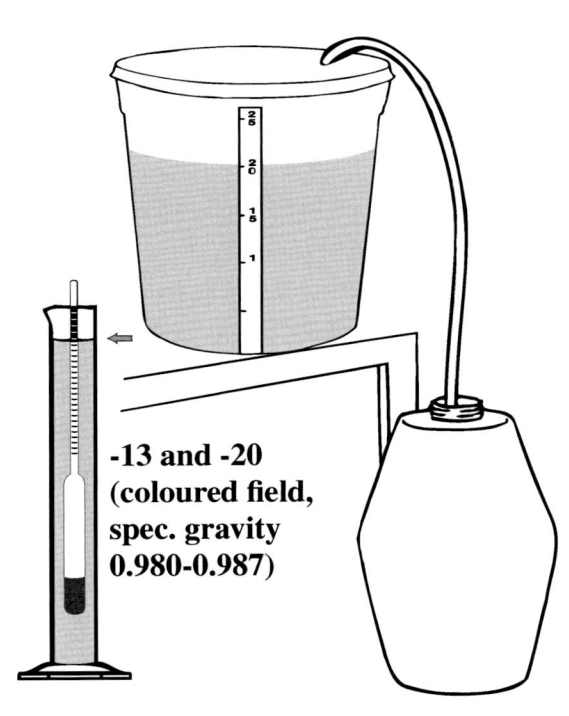

20–25°C

-13 and -20 (coloured field, spec. gravity 0.980-0.987)

5. TRANSFERRING

When the fermentation has stopped, take a reading with the hydrometer. This should read between -13 and -20 (coloured field, spec. gravity 0.980-0.987).

If the mash is crystal clear transfer to the distillation vessel, if the mash has not cleared, transfer to another vessel. Ensure the lees are left behind. Then simply wait a few days and the mash will clear. If time is a problem use a wine clearing agent.

Transfer the clear mash to the distillation apparatus, ensuring the lees are left behind.

Mash fermentation with baker´s yeast

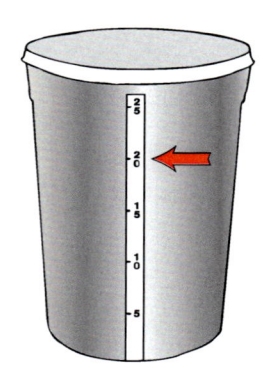

1. MARK OUT THE VOLUME

Make a level mark on the fermentation vessel showing how many Litres is to be fermented. Remember to leave at least 200 mm for foaming.

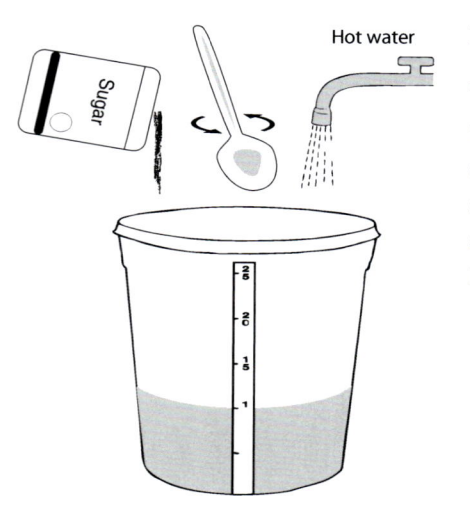

2. MIXING

Transfer 10 Litres of hot water from the hot water tap. Add the sugar. Shake or stir until the sugar is completely dissolved. **NOTE:** sugar must be completely dissolved to be fermented to alcohol.

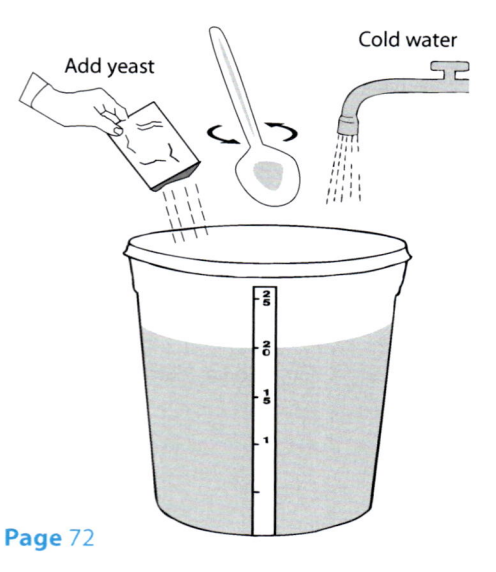

3. ADD YEAST

Fill up the fermentation vessel with cold water, preferably oxygen rich water from a spray head. Fill to the level mark. Add 100 to 250 grams of fresh baker's yeast for 25 Litres and yeast nutrients. If fresh baker's yeast is used, dissolve in a tea cup of granulated sugar, and add 2 decilitres of water first. Shake to mix well. Put the cover on without using the fermentation lock.

4. FERMENTATION

20–25°C

Fit the fermentation lock, with water in it, after 2 days fermentation, and press tight the cover. If water escapes from the fermentation lock, because of the speed of the fermentation, wait one to two days before refilling.

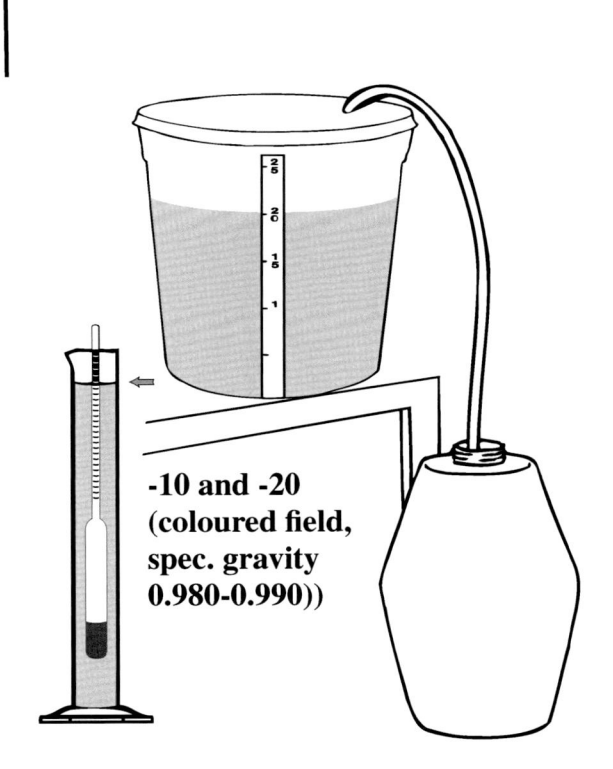

-10 and -20 (coloured field, spec. gravity 0.980-0.990))

5. TRANSFERRING

When the fermentation has stopped, take a reading with the hydrometer. This should read approximately between -10 and -20 (coloured field, spec. gravity 0.980-0.990).

If the mash is crystal clear transfer to the distillation vessel, if the mash has not cleared, transfer to another vessel. Ensure the lees are left behind. Then simply wait a few days and the mash will clear. If time is a problem use a wine clearing agent. This will work between 4 and 24 hours.

Transfer the clear mash to the distillation apparatus, ensuring the lees are left behind.

Distillation

The principle of distillation is that one heats up the mash to boiling point, and then you cool down the steam (condensation) to a liquid. Alcohol has a lower boiling point (78.3°C) than water (100°C) and so boils first. By this means the alcohol is separated from the mash.

The strongest alcohol you can achieve by distillation is 95%. This is because a mixture of 95% alcohol and 5% of water has a lower boiling point of (78.15°C) then 100% alcohol (which is 78.3°C). This is called an azeotrope.

Effect of atmospheric pressure on boiling points

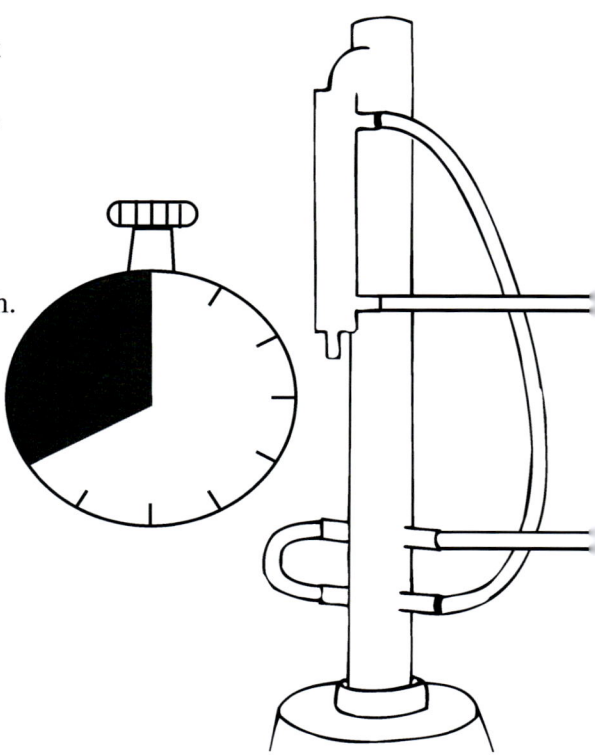

Pressure

psi	mm Hg	inches Hg	kPa	millibars	Elevation Feet	Ethanol95 °C	Water 25°C
16.5	853	33.6	113.7	1137	- 3280	81.2	103.3
15.6	806	31.8	107.5	1075	- 1640	79.7	101.7
14.7	760	29.9	101.3	1013	Sea level	78.15	100.0
13.9	716	28.2	95.4	954	1640	76.5	98.3
13.0	674	26.5	89.8	898	3281	74.9	96.7
12.3	634	25.0	84.5	845	4921	73.3	95.0

You can also use the on-line boiling point calculator at www.partyman.se/calculator.html.

Re-distillation

As a rule only one distillation is required if activated carbon is used. If one wish to distil twice usually one distils once quickly, dilutes the resultant distillate with water to 50% and redistills. The second time should be slower and more accurate (at 78°C).

After this the alcohol should be diluted to a maximum of 50%, or preferably 42-45% and is then filtered through activated carbon. This gives a very satisfactory result and the first distillation is done very quickly. If one wishes to distil twice with better results, the best is to double distil as perfectly as possible at the correct temperature for the initial distillation and then dilute to 42-45% (activated carbon has its maximum purifying effect at about 42% alcohol) and purified through **wet** activated carbon according to my instructions.

Before the second distillation you should wash the boiling vessel and distillation column thoroughly. You should also extra carefully wash the column fillings using a good cleaning agent like **Glasrens** (partymanshop.com/glasrens-cleans-and-sterilizes-100-grams.html), **HLSC**, or another good sterilising cleaner.

Then the spirit should be redistilled at exactly the right temperature. This will give you a pure strong alcohol (95%), because the distillate has already been purified in activated carbon.

A prerequisite for pure alcohol is that the column has been thoroughly cleaned so that the spirit cannot acquire off-flavours from old deposits. Towards the end of the distillation process the alcohol content drops despite its being very pure, so if one wants 95% alcohol this should be kept separate.

If this alcohol is to be diluted to normal strength spirit one should filter it through activated carbon to remove any small traces of impurities that may remain.

Fractional distillation

The slower one distils the mash, the purer the alcohol will be.

To obtain as pure a spirit as possible, one should use a still with a distillation column. A column is a vertical tube that extends 590mm or more from the boiling vessel. The column is usually filled with unsymmetrical fillings with as large a surface area as possible. The vapour passes up through the column until it is cooled down to a liquid alcohol. Boiling takes place all the way up the column. Because of the differing boiling points of water and alcohol a separation of these occurs in the column - which is termed fractionation.

The temperature at the base of the column becomes the same as that of the boiling vessel (towards that of water, 100°C) and the temperature at the top is regulated by the heat source to 78°C.

95%	78,15°C
94%	
93%	
91%	79°C
89%	79,2°C
80%	79,9°C
47%	83,1°C
7%	94,5°C

Mash 0,6%
99,5°C

Passing from the bottom to the top the temperature drops off all the way up. So the mash (water) with a higher boiling point condenses and runs back down into the boiling vessel, whereas the alcohol gets through without condensing. One can further improve the column by fitting 2 or 3 thin tubes through it, through which cold water passes through. The tubes cool down the column filling, and by this through-cooling, water and fusel oil are separated extremely effectively by faster condensation on the cooled filling.

By regulating the speed of the cooling water one can regulate the temperature in the top of the column. With more powerful cooling (increased water flow) the temperature cools and lowering the cooling effect raises the temperature. This means that one is independent of a step-less heat control for the still. One sets the heat source roughly, and adjusts with precision using the amount of cooling water running through the column.

The taller the column the more effective is the fractionalisation. But for home distilling only a 590 mm (2 foot) long column is needed. A longer column only fractionally improves the results.

Note: if there are no cooling tubes through the column, the length of the column needs to be 20 times the width, and not less than 3-4 feet. One distillation, with a distillation unit with a column, corresponds to eight ordinary distillations.

After the column is located a condensation cooler where the alcohol is condensed to liquid form. Distillation gives best results with the distillation temperature set to the boiling point at the take of point. **The boiling point of 95% alcohol is 78.15°C.** 78.15°C is the temperature that produces the best distillate.

If you use a boiling plate connected directly to a power source, for the distillation apparatus, you can use a stepless heat power regulator (triac) between the socket and the boiling plate. This gives control of the heat, and the boiling plate can be set on maximum. During the initial heating up stage, the regulator should not be used. It should be connected when the column has become hot, about 150 mm above the still. If you have too little cooling water, and a low heat, the apparatus will be affected quite easily by a draught from an open door or window. If this occurs, increase the heat and water supply slightly, so that the distillation becomes more stable at the same head temperature. Distillation apparatus should be located in a draught-free place.

The first drops of distillate to emerge (fore shots) are primarily comprised of acetaldehyde. Acetal is also present, a product very similar to acetaldehyde. So-called aromatics are also present. They are not toxic but taste will be considerably improved if they are discarded.

There is **no methanol** (or only **traces** of methanol) when fermenting **sugar**. In whisky there is always a small percentage of methanol (from cereal fermentation), but it is not poisonous when drunk together with alcohol – because alcohol is the cure for methanol poisoning. But, when making whisky, it is common to throw away the first 50 millilitres of fore shot, as it contains mostly methanol. As methanol has a lower boiling point then alcohol.

When we have finished the distillation process, the apparatus should be allowed to cool and the mash should be emptied down the toilet (hot mash has a foul smell). If the apparatus is allowed to stand and cool one must never block the outlet for the distillate.

It is easy to get a kink in the tube from which the distillate emerges. If this outlet is blocked during cooling a vacuum is formed in the boiling vessel. This is because the warm air and mash shrink as they cool and takes up considerably less volume. If the boiling vessel is made of glass this under pressure will cause it to implode.

If it is made of stainless steel it will be screwed up like a steel rag. To avoid imploding, the thermometer, the connection between the column, and boiling vessel should ALWAYS be released after the distillation process. This is to allow air to enter, so the pressure is equalised within the still and the column.

How to distil extra pure alcohol

First distil 20 - 25 Litres of mash once, and dilute the alcohol to 40-50%. Then redistill this alcohol. Throw away the first 20 millilitres. Lower the temperature so the distillate drops very slowly. Put away the first 300-400 millilitres (head) for redistilling. You will collect 2 Litres of alcohol (at approx. 95%) when distilling as slow as possible. This will take 15-20 hours. Take away the rest (tail) for re-distillation. Your 2 Litres of alcohol will need only a little activated carbon for
purification. If one wants to produce 95% pure alcohol, this is possible but there is more work (example: more hours equilibrating the column).

Note: distilling 95% pure alcohol by equilibrated distillation must always be done in two steps. First, strip the mash. Then dilute to 40-50% alcohol. Now you may do the equilibrated distillation.

It is impossible (in practice) to make a totally pure 95% alcohol, from mash, in one step. Since there will always be some sort of off smell and off flavour from the fore shots - from the column, or from old deposits in column filling.

The Amazing Plastic Still
A clever method of making spirit

The Amazing Method

Firstly distil with a still, discharge the first 20 millilitres, and dilute alcohol to 25-30%.

Then use **The Amazing Still**. This still does **not** distil – it vaporises. The process needs no cooling and maintains itself. It takes days because process is slow, but The Amazing Still produces a **very** pure alcohol. This method can also be used the other way by first using The Amazing Still, and secondly using a column still.

www.amazingstill.com

Temperature

The slower the distillation the purer the spirit will be. To achieve maximum quality, the temperature of the thermometer, on the top of the column, should read 78°C (+/- 0.2°C). The temperature is regulated by the supply of heat under the distillation vessel, and by regulating the flow of the cooling water. Rough adjustments should be made with the heater, and fine adjustments with the cooling water flow rate. A correctly adjusted distillation apparatus (if it has cooling tubes through the column) does not require any attention.

The distillate holds to 85% or more. When the spirit is exhausted no more is released from the apparatus. The temperature falls in the column, and the mash condenses and runs back into the boiling vessel. The heat source must not have a thermostat as it is not then possible to set the temperature so the mash surge boils up the column. With elements built into the boiling vessel, the initial rapid heating can be made with several elements and then distilling can be done with one or two heating elements.

Effect of atmospheric pressure on boiling points

The boiling point (the temperature at which a liquid boils) is influenced by the temperature at which the vapour pressure of the liquid equals the atmospheric pressure at sea level (760 mm Hg). In reality, the atmospheric pressure changes daily with weather and elevation. Not even if one lives at sea level will there be a stable pressure of 760 mm Hg. This affects both the boiling point of water (if you test run it, a thermometer shows 100C in boiling water) and the boiling point of alcohol, for us the azeotrope of 95% alcohol and 5% water, 78.15C. We can use this phenomenon to do vacuum distillation as well. When pressure lowers, the boiling point decreases, and when pressure is higher, the boiling point increases. Atmospheric pressure is measured with a barometer. For conversions, you can use the chart shown in this book or use the online boiling point calculator at www.partyman.se.

Column 1		Column 2		Column 3	
95%	78,15°C	95%	78,15°C	95%	78,15°C
95%	78,15°C	95%	78,15°C	94%	
95%	78,15°C	94%		93%	
94%		93%		91%	79°C
93%		91%	79°C	89%	79,2°C
91%	79°C	87%	79,3°C	80%	79,9°C
86%	79,4°C	62%	81,5°C	47%	83,1°C
57%	82°C	13%	91,1°C	7%	94,5°C
Boiling mash 10% 92,6°C		**Mash 1% 99°C**		**Mash 0,6% 99,5°C**	

Theoretical thresholds in a distillation column

There are 8 thresholds in the distillation column of a proper home distillation apparatus. Here the thresholds have been simplified for the sake of clarity.

The actual location of the thresholds

In reality there is quite some distance between the two first thresholds and very little between the last. This means, that if one only raises the heat up a little to move the thresholds, one can drive out the top 6-7 thresholds and get a weaker impure spirit. This illustrates the importance of keeping the temperature accurate. If the temperature is held the thresholds are kept in place.

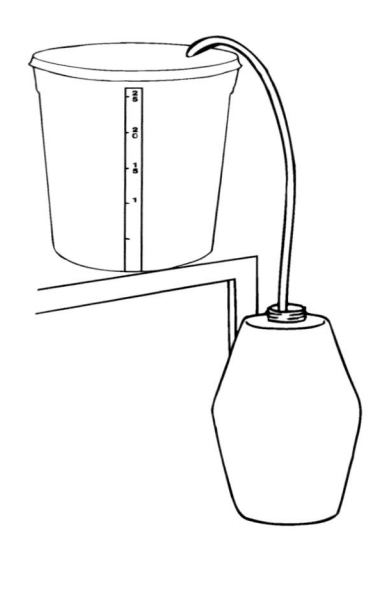

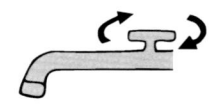

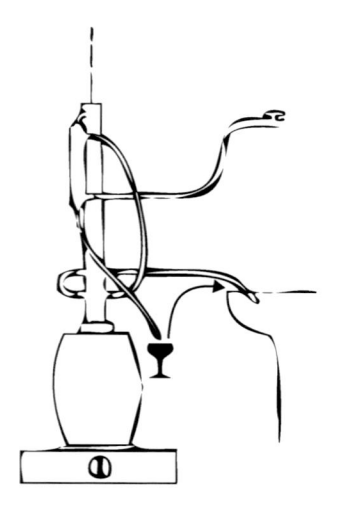

Distillation procedure

1. We transfer the crystal clear mash to the boiling vessel using a siphon without disturbing the lees.

The boiling vessel must not be filled right up, allow a minimum of 200 mm for boiling. The mash expands when it is heated, and the spare volume is necessary for this.

2. The distilling apparatus should be assembled, and the cooling water connected up. The cooling water only needs to run slowly.

In between 1 to 3 hours (depending on mash volume and boiling plate capacity) the distillation starts. The first 20 millilitres should be thrown away as they are comprised mainly of by-products (including aldehydes), which are formed during fermentation. These can be most accurately described as scent-like substances, and they have a boiling point of about 65°C. They are entirely harmless, and can be retained, but the flavour will be improved if they are not included.

3. Now set the temperature at the column head. This is done by roughly setting the heat source, and a fine adjustment of the cooling water. Try to set at 78°C. It is imperative that the temperature is under 80°C.

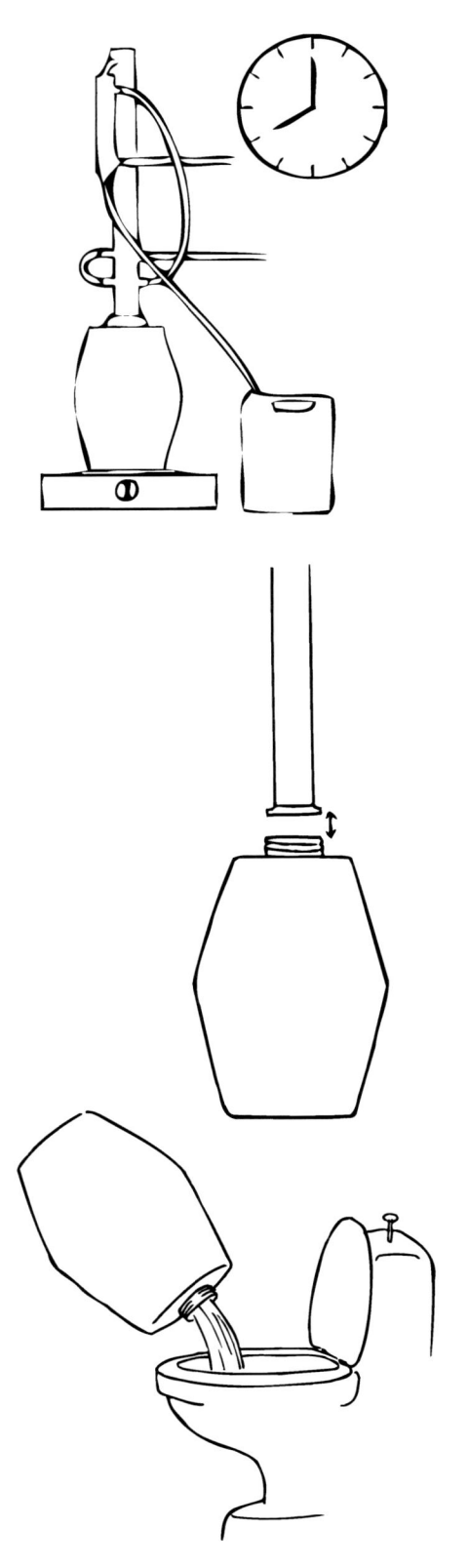

4. After between 8 to 12 hours distillation, it is time to finish the process. Exactly when the process is finished will be decided by the temperature at the column head. Either the temperature rises, so one switches off at 90°C, or the temperature falls 10-20°C (or more) and the spirit **stops dripping** from the apparatus.

This is because one has succeeded in setting the temperature so accurately that all the alcohol all gone from the mash and the vapour cannot get through the column. From a batch of 22-25 Litres of mash, one should be able to produce 2 to 2 and 3/4 Litres of 90-95% concentrated alcohol. In practice this means 4-6 Litres of 40-45% spirit (more with the use of Turbo Yeast).

5. Undo the connector between the column and the boiling vessel and set aside the apparatus to cool. Air **must** be allowed into the vessel; otherwise the resultant vacuum can cause the boiling vessel to implode.

6. When the mash has cooled pour it out into the lavatory. Rinse out the vessel and reverse rinse the column. Use a good detergent when washing the boiling vessel, column, and column filling.

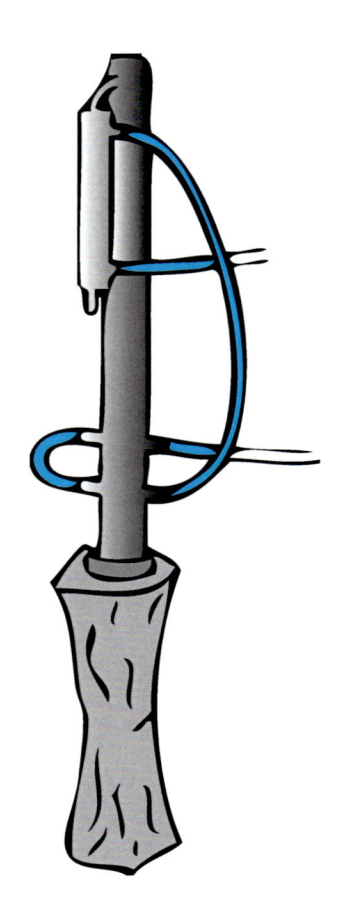

SAFETY: Danger of accidents and other important points

Implosion of the boiling vessel can occur. After distillation, the mash cools in the boiling vessel, and a vacuum forms. Air cannot get into the vessel through the column in time (the hose could also be twisted) so the boiling vessel implodes, shrinking like a rag.

Following completion of the distillation the thermometer should be disconnected, and the connection between the vessel, and the column should be unfastened immediately. This allows the entry of air. The forming of the vacuum begins as soon as the heat is turned off.

Explosions

Explosions have also occurred. This is nearly always when mixing chemical mash comprising ethyl acetate and sodium hydroxide. Alcohol in gaseous form (the mixture gets hot) spreads into the air.

The gas formation is ignited by an open flame or a spark, such as from a thermostat.

Alcohol vapour can leak from a distillation apparatus in a few ways. The column can leak from a badly welded joint, or something is not tightly connected enough, or distillation has started without the cooling water tap being turned on. When one has built a distilling column and/or still, the column should be mounted on the still and tested. You can do this by placing it under water, and connecting a source of compressed air to the outlet of the condensation cooler, to ensure that there are no leaks. If there are any leaks the air will bubble through the water.

Note: one must always make a test run with water before using the still for alcohol distillation.

This is done to ensure that the still functions properly, and it will also clean the still before use. If the apparatus leaks or the cooling hose jumps off, pure alcohol vapour will enter the room when you use the still. Therefore cooling water must be turned on from the beginning, equipment must be in good condition, and all hoses fastened with hose clips.

Absolutely no provisional (ad-hoc, short-term, quick & dirty) solutions should be allowed in connecting the cooling hoses to the equipment, or the cold water tap. If alcohol vapours do leak the smell will be immediately apparent.

Risk of fire

Risk of fire is not relevant as we use electric heating. There have been cases where heating has been speeded up by the use of open flame propane, butane, natural gas, or spirit heaters. The first 20 millilitres of output have been measured off, and then the distillation has progressed unattended, with the cooling water on. All is well until the container has filled up, and the alcohol has spilled over into the open flame, igniting. Therefore you should only use electricity.

Flooding

Flooding can arise if the cooling water hose jumps off.

All cooling water hoses must be properly fitted with hose clips. There must also be a proper coupling between the tap and the cooling water hose. The cooling water discharge must be fixed properly and connected or fixed to the sink, or a drain.

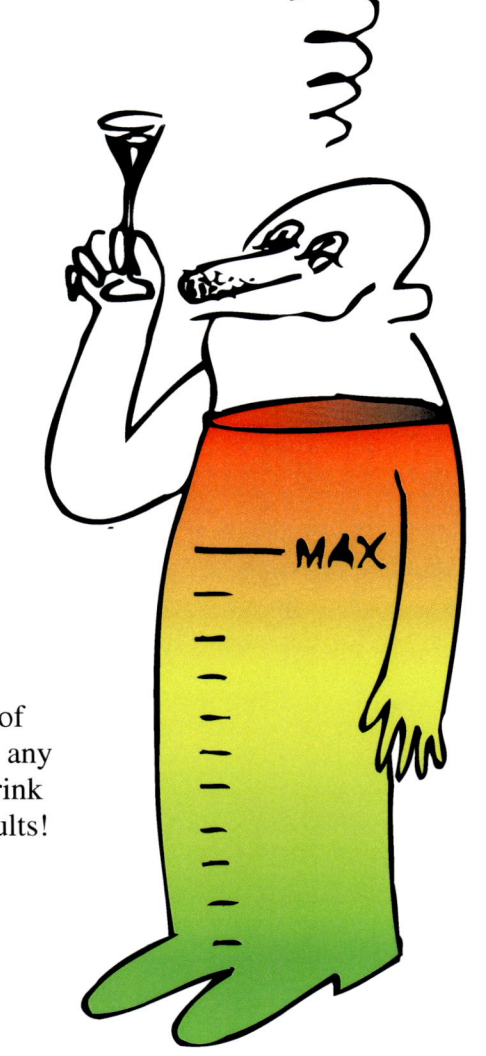

Poisoning

Poisoning from spirit can never occur. Not even impure spirit is toxic; it just tastes bad because of the fusel oil (which exacerbates any hangover). However, one can drink too much, with well-known results!

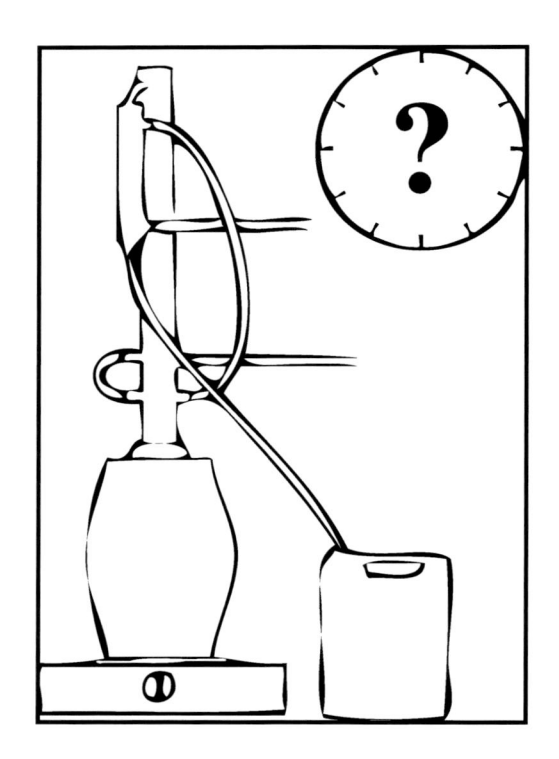

Trouble shooting - Distillation fails to start

Check that the heating is on. Check that the heat source has sufficient capacity, and is set fully on. It can take several hours to heat up the mash. Ask yourself is there mash in the boiling vessel? Is there free passage for the steam/distillate through the column, cooler and hose?

Contaminated spirit flows from the apparatus?

Too much mash in the boiling vessel. Pour some off.

Spirit comes out, but it is not clear?

The column filling is dirty or homemade. Clean or change.

Too much mash in the boiling vessel?

Pour some off.

The mash surge boils?

There can be a thermostat on the heater. Remove it or change the heating source.

The cooling water hose is reversed. Check against the sketch in this book.

There could be too much mash in the boiling vessel. Allow for at least 200 mm space. Add some antifoaming agent (for example M10 Stabile).

If you have water pump water pressure can vary which can cause surge boiling. There are several solutions to this.

Alcohol is too weak?

The temperature is too high in the column. Lower to 78°C.

Too little output?

At least 10-13% of the amount of mash should come out, giving alcohol of 84-95%. If less appears it is nearly always because the mash has not been fully fermented. This is usually due to poor Turbo Yeast (it is very tempting for a producer to mix baker's yeast and diammonium phosphate at a very low cost and sell at the same price as real Turbo Yeast). This can be avoided by only using well-known brands.

Always check the mash with the hydrometer before distilling. It should read on the minus scale (coloured field -13 to -20 Oechsle or s.g. 0.980 to 0.987). It is meaningless to add more sugar than the yeast can handle.

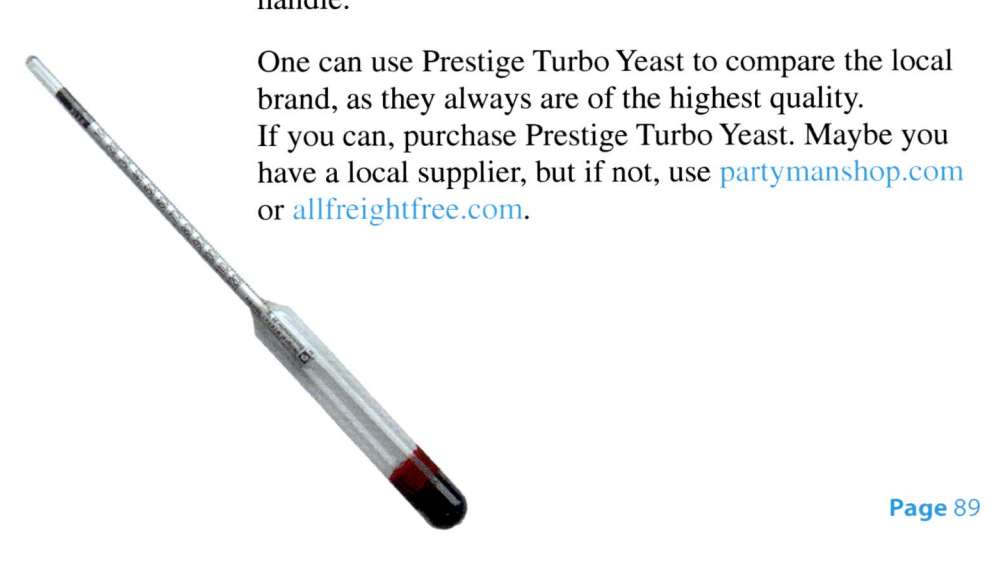

One can use Prestige Turbo Yeast to compare the local brand, as they always are of the highest quality.
If you can, purchase Prestige Turbo Yeast. Maybe you have a local supplier, but if not, use partymanshop.com or allfreightfree.com.

Dilution

Calculation of the amount of concentrated alcohol is required to make up 75 cl of spirit, or liqueur, to a particular strength. When working with 95% spirit and one wishes to impart a particular strength to the liquor being blended it is calculated in the following way (in this case for a 30% strength):

Volume (Litres) x required alcohol strength x 1.05
(1 : 0.95 = conversion of 95% alcohol to 100% alcohol for the purpose of calculation) = 0.75 x 0.30 x 1.05 = 0.236
(236 millilitres - use a measuring beaker).

If spirit with another strength is used (for example 80%) then calculate thus:

1: 0.80 = 1.25. this gives us the figure that converts the 80% alcohol to 100% alcohol for the purpose of calculation.

This method of calculation can be used to work out any strength of alcohol (just a case of changing the % value).

Then: Volume in Litres (0.75) x required alcohol %
(30) x 1.25 = 281. 281 millilitres of 80% spirits should be used.

It is, however, much easier to use the free online calculator at:

distillery-yeast.com/distillery-tips/converters/#blanda_alkohol

When the alcohol content is being reduced one must ensure that there is room for the sugar and essence when blending liqueurs. For example, it is not possible to blend a 40% liqueur using a 45% alcohol as there will be no room for the sugar. If the volume is not made up fully when mixing sugar syrup, essence, and alcohol, the remainder is filled out with distilled or softened water.

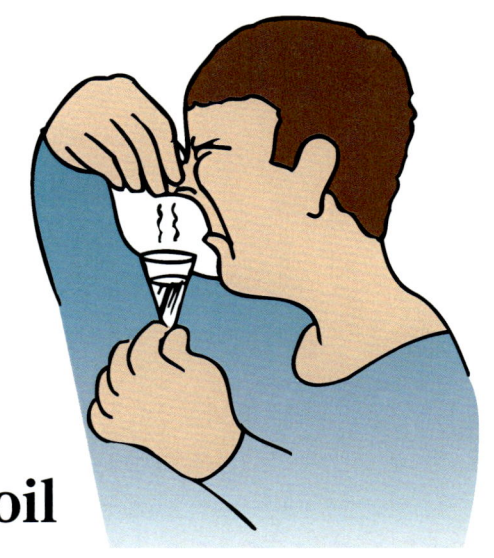

Fusel oil - Facts about fusel oil

Fusel oil is the common name for by-products as well as higher alcohols formed in the fermentation process. The principal ingredient of fusel oil is amylalcohol which comprises 65 to 80% of fusel oil. It comprises all forms of isobutylcarbinol and amylalcohol. It also contains 15-25% of isobutyl- and approximately 4-7% of n-propyl alcohol. Amyl-, butyl- and propylalcohols comprise the principal components of fusel oils, but there are other substances although none of these is present in significant quantities. They appear in such small amounts that one needs only consider the principal components.

The makeup of fusel oil depends principally on the ingredients of the fermentation and the fermentation temperature, and fusel oil is the aroma of the mash. For example, in brandy and other fruit-base spirits (for example slivovitz, calvados, etc.) the fusel oil content is 0.6% or more. This is the principal aroma of the drink and after storage and maturing most of the fusel oil constituents have taken the form of esters. In basic raw spirit distilled from mash based on sugar the fusel content is usually between 0.4 and 0.7% of the 95% alcohol. In an experiment with 200 grams of sugar in 2 Litres of water and using 40 grams of baker's yeast the fusel content of the raw spirit was 0.40%. As this mash was no more than 6% one must reckon with more fusel in practice (despite the overdose of yeast in the experiment).

The addition of ammonium salts (nitrogen) to the mash reduces the formation of fusel oil, i.e. yeast nutrient salt (diammonium phosphate), or the use of a Turbo Yeast. Then the results are purified using activated carbon.

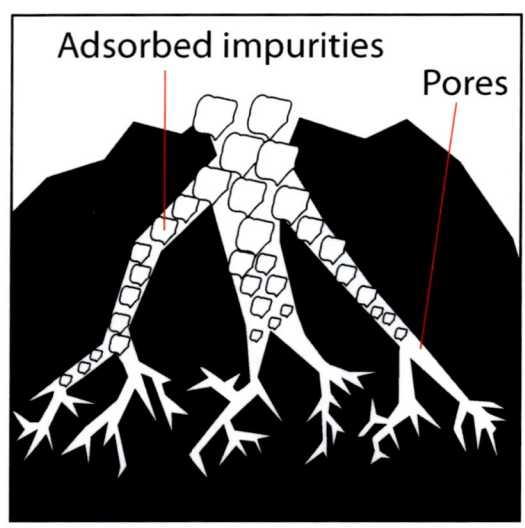

Purification using activated carbon

Purification of the spirit is the most important thing in the entire manufacturing process. It is principally down to purification for the best results. The purification method I describe is the **only** method that gives an absolutely pure spirit. If a good small grain sized activated carbon is used then 1.7 liters (0,5-1 kg) is sufficient for 4-5 Litres of spirit (diluted to under 50%) or more. The same purification method is used around the world. The only difference is that commercial spirits manufacturers filter the spirit from below, percolating upwards, with a constant flow rate of the spirit. This is in order to be able to precisely control the filtering at a speed of 0.25 HSV/hourly space per volume.

Activated carbon can be compared to small sponges full of holes. The absorption capacity of the activated carbon is measured in the area of these holes per gram (expressed in m2/gram). The grain size of the activated carbon determines how fast it absorbs impurities. Effective activated carbon should have a grain size of a maximum of approximately 1 mm. Larger grain sizes work too ineffectively, and are unable to use the surface area inside the grain. Powdered carbon **cannot** be used for the best purification method as the powder consolidates and blocks the process. The impurities are absorbed by the pores in the activated carbon, including fusel oils and the flavour of the yeast. To take best advantage of the pores one filters slowly through a highly **wet** layer of activated carbon (1.5 metres).

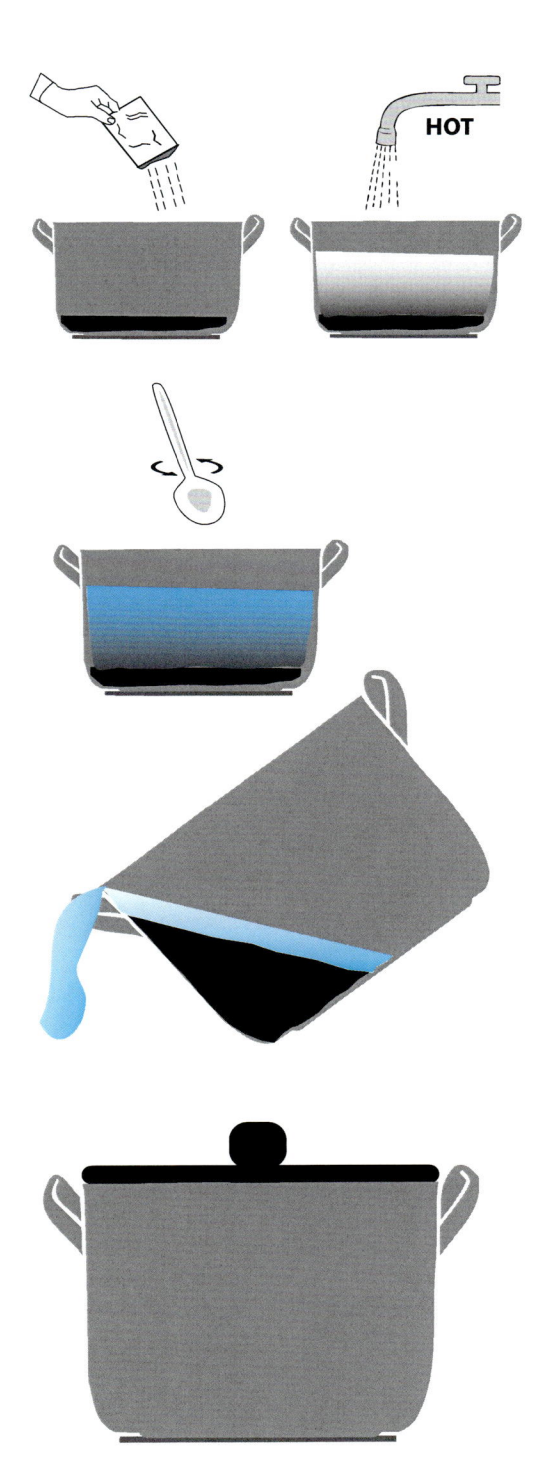

Procedure

1. Pour the granulated carbon into a stainless steel saucepan, and then fill up with double the amount of hot or boiling water.

2. Stir with a large spoon allowing the carbon to sink to the bottom of the saucepan before discarding the surplus water. Repeat the process 4 or 5 times, making sure all soluble substances in the carbon have been washed out.

Cover with boiling water, put a lid on the saucepan, and leave it to soak for 24 hours. It is the internal wetting within the carbon granule that mostly increases the purification effect. After 24 hours add 100% more, so we can use the whole capacity of the activated carbon.

3. Discard surplus water, and cover once more with hot or boiling water.

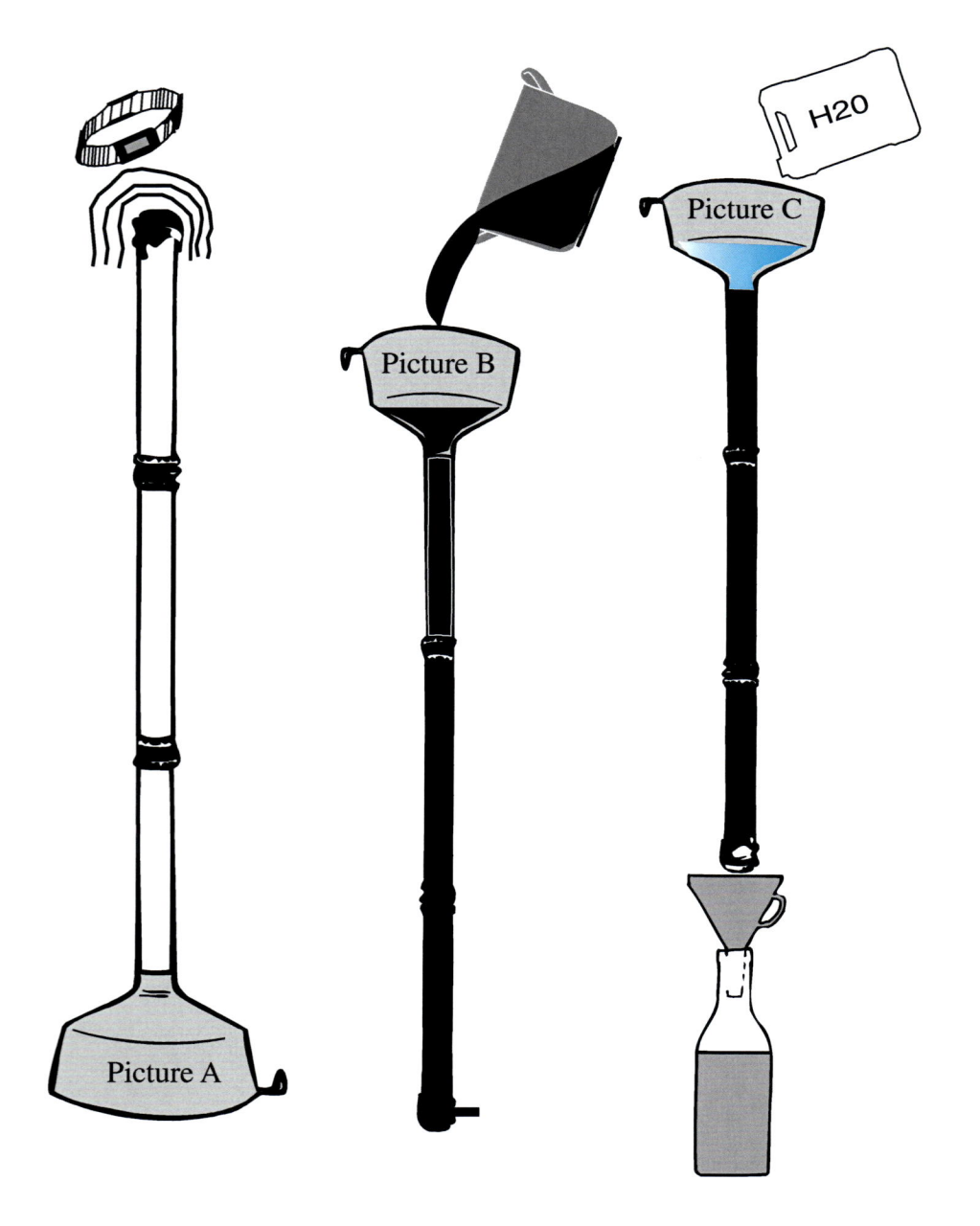

4. Stir and pour off remaining water.

5. Attach 2 or 3 filters to the tube (Picture A), and fill completely with warm water. Fill up with carbon, making sure it is poured into the water, and all air is expelled (Picture B). Tap the tube to settle and pack the carbon. Filter 2 to 5 Litres of water through the tube to flush out the remaining soluble substances (Picture C).

42-50%

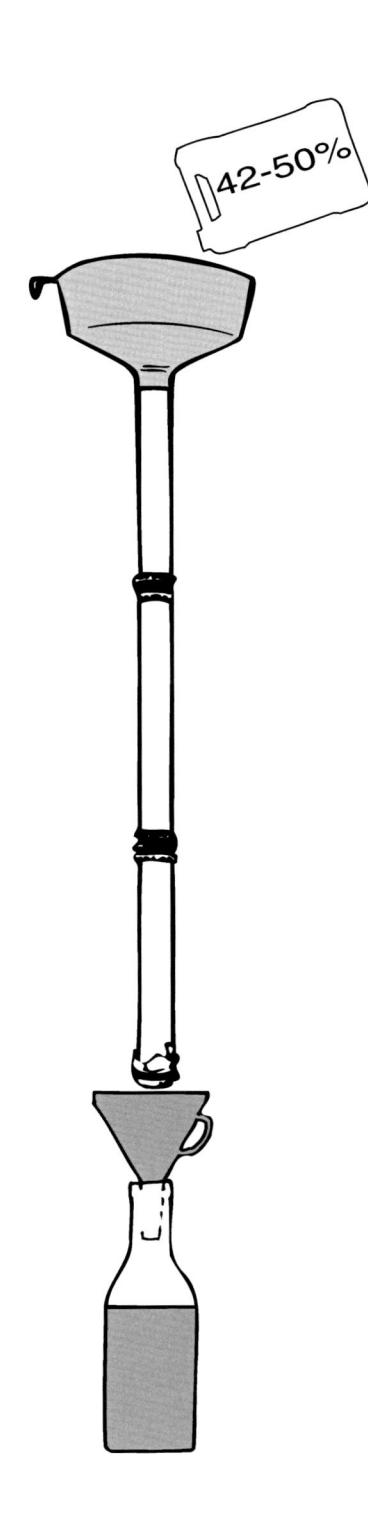

6. Pour in alcohol as the last drops of water drain from the funnel. Taste the filtered water/alcohol, and as soon as the alcohol emerges, let it run into a container. Cover the funnel with a lid to avoid vaporization of the alcohol.

7. When the last drops of alcohol leave the funnel, pour in a litre of water to ensure that all alcohol is filtered through. Again, taste the filtered alcohol/water, and discard the water.

8. This way, the carbon has started, and all the air in the tube has expelled. It also eliminates the bypass "channels" formed when using dry carbon, and prevents changes in the pH-value (from 7 to 10) that normally occur when the soluble substances in the carbon are dissolved in water or alcohol.

Once the carbon has been heated and soaked, and when all air is expelled from the tube, the alcohol will flow through the channels in the carbon, and not escape unfiltered.

Effectiveness is increased by at least 100%, giving a cleaner alcohol and it is possible to filter twice the volume. The diameter of the tube should not be less than 35 mm. If it is, too much alcohol escapes unfiltered along the inner wall (wall effect).

Activated Carbon Filtration Unit

- Large funnel

- Pipe filled with wet activated carbon

- Height 1.5 metres

- Diameter 38 mm or more

- Filter paper fixed with stainless steel jubilee clip.

Purification using the same activated carbon twice

If one purifies spirit through activated carbon in a pipe, and then passes the same spirit twice or more through the same pipe, the result will be **deterioration**. This is because the pipe method, apart from giving excellent absorption of impurities, has a further function. Some of the impurities are loosely bound to the surface of carbon granules (activated carbon has a charge that attracts impurities). Most are caught at the top of the pipe, and a smaller amount at the pipes base.

This is one of the reasons why the pipe method (percolation through a highly granulated active carbon layer) is **superior** to all other activated carbon filtering methods. So, if the same spirit is passed through again, the impurities are pulled down a bit further, and some come out with the spirit. Double filtration using the same activated carbon gives **inferior** results.

Purification must be perfect

Purification must be perfect. Carbon has the capacity to purify the spirit so that it is **entirely free** from off-tastes and bad odours. If the spirit is not perfect it must be purified again.

Badly purified spirit (off tasting from fusel oil) will have a flavour conflict when mixed with certain essences. If one mixes an essence called Hunters Schnapps (which tastes like Jagermeister) with a poor spirit it will taste terrible. This will apply to most flavours. However certain flavours, such as whisky, dark rum, brandy, and bitters, can accommodate some off flavours and still taste good.

Free eBook about activated carbon

At partyman.se/free_ebook.html one can download a 28 page free e-book about activated carbon. Highly recommended, it explains everything. However, this book is a little boring, as it has so much detailed content and it is not an essential read.

Different brands of activated carbon

There are not many brands that are suitable for alcohol purification. There is also a big quality difference from one delivery to next, especially on coconut-based carbon. I recommend using The Prestige Activated Stone Carbon (Size 0.4 – 0.85 mm). It is good quality, and it is exported world-wide. If you want to try other brands you will have something to compare with.

Note: you must **wet** granulated activated carbon before use. Otherwise you will only be able to purify between 20 to 50% of the alcohol. For best results pre wet your activated carbon!

Blending with essences

Here follows some advice on the procedure for getting the best results when blending spirits and liqueurs.

Basic prerequisites:

- Only use the best quality spirit without off tasting flavours.

- Only use neutral soft chlorine-free water, which does not contain manganese salts and iron.

- Only the best essences of the highest quality must be used.

- For liqueurs only use the best, absolutely clear, sugar syrup made from the finest sugar. The sugar syrup must not suffer from the "boiled sugar taste" and must not have burned.

- At least 6-8 weeks maturation before consumption.

- Whisky must have 5 to 10% real whisky added, in order to achieve a good quality taste.

- Accuracy and exact attention to detail during blending.

These are the basic prerequisites for a good product. In particular, the quality of the spirit and the water for mixing is important. The hardness of the water is also extremely important. The different forms of chalk, iron, and magnesium salt, are the substances creating the degree of hardness in the water. They are much more soluble in water than in alcohol. If alcohol is added to hard water the chalk and salts fall out of solution. The fall from solution is faster the greater the level of alcohol content.

The home blender can avoid this problem by using distilled water, but for the commercial manufacturer find it more economical to use softened well water. If a small amount is saved from each litre used, this becomes a considerable sum for a year's production for a medium, or large liqueur manufacturer.

In the case of liqueurs one uses 96% spirit and ready mixed absolutely clear filtered sugar syrup. Granulated sugar contains small particles that can float about in the liqueur when one mixes oneself. But it is not more difficult than simply filtering the syrup to remove the particles through a sieve or cloth. Commercial manufacturers filter the product one last time before bottling. For the home blender it can be an advantage to dissolve the sugar directly in the spirit.

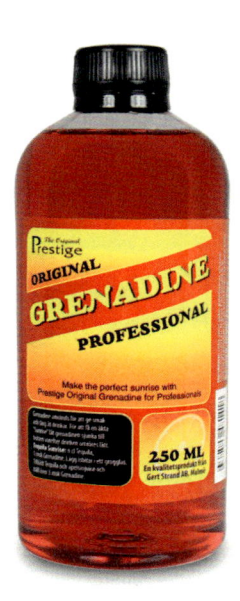

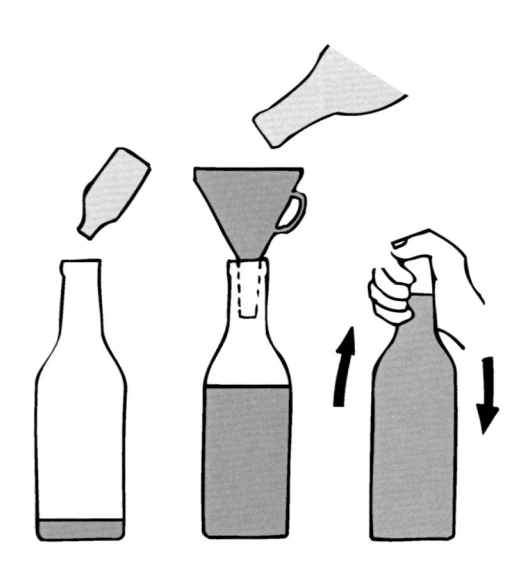

Blending with spirit essences

Pour the essence in an empty bottle and fill three-quarters full with spirit. Shake the bottle. Fill up and shake again. Allow the bottle to lie according to type of drink. Even types that do not require laying down (e.g. gin, aquavit, rum, etc.) should be kept overnight, or preferably for some days. Storing improves the flavour, although the improvement is often marginal.

Blending with liqueur essences

Pour the essence and sugar into an empty bottle. Fill the bottle three quarters full with spirit and shake until the sugar is completely dissolved. Fill up and shake again.

Formula for calculating dilution

How much spirit should you use when diluting for alcohol strength?

Required alcohol strength x volume required:
Alcohol content (%) of the alcohol strength = how many cl strong alcohol we need.

Example: We have spirit at 60% and wish to make a 75 cl liqueur of 25% alcohol content: 25 x 75 : 60 = 31. We must use 31 cl of 60% spirit.

Begin with the spirit; add the essence, sugar and water. When a volume of 75 cl is reached the required alcoholic strength will be correct.

Tips: there is an online calculator for this at:
distillery-yeast.com/distillery-tips/converters/#blanda_alkohol.

Table of original alcohol content of liqueurs

Advokaat / Yellow egg liqueur / 15%
Apricot brandy / Light brown / 29%
Benedictine / Golden brown herbal liqueur / 40%
Blackberry Liqueur / Red / 27%
Creme De Cacao / Brown / 25%
Creme De Cacao / White / 25%
Cherry Brandy / Red / 25%
Chocomint / Brown / 27%
Cointreau / White / 40%
Cordial MÇdoc / Red fruit liqueur / 38%
Creme De Bananas / Light yellow / 29%
Creme De Cassis Dark / Red / 24%
Curacao / Brown / 40%
Curacao / Green / 34%
Curacao / Orange / 32%
Cusenier Orange / Light brown / 40%
Drambuie / Whisky liqueur / 40%
Grand Marnier Jaune / Light golden / 38%
Grand Marnier Rouge / Red brown / 38%
Green Chartreause / Herbal liqueur / 55%
Yellow Chartreause / Herbal liqueur / 40%
Coffee Liqueur / Brown / 26%
Kahlua / Brown coffee / 26%
Kaptenlojtnant / Swedish liqueur / 40%
Kloster Likor / Swedish liqueur / 43%
Lakka / Finnish cloudberry liqueur / 28%
Licor 43 / Golden herbal liqueur / 43%
Mandarin / Orange / 25%
Marachino / White cherry liqueur / 32%
Parfait l'Amour / Violet / 29%
Pernod / Liqorice / 31%
Slivovitz / Plum brandy / 30%

Original gravity of liqueurs

Peppermint / White or green / 30%
Peter Heering / Cherry brandy / 24%
Poire William / Pear brandy / 30%
Polar / Red / 29%
Royal triple sec / White Curacao / 39%
Seve fournier / Light brown / 38%
Strega / Yellow / 40%
Tia Maria / Brown / 31%

Original gravity of aperitifs and bitters

Underberg / 49%
Angostura Bitters / 45%
Fernet Branca / 40%
Campari / 21%
Ouzo / Liquorice / 40%
Rikard / Liquorice / 31%

The alcohol strengths given above are based on the strength of the products as sold in Sweden. Local tax laws (excise duty, etc.) can affect the alcohol content for a particular market. A home distiller can change the strength of their drinks for their own taste.
Taxes do affect the strength of alcohol in drinks.
In Sweden most vodka is now 38%, whisky 40%.
In Denmark most liquor is 37.5%. This is because of an alcohol tax in Sweden that makes higher alcohol content more expensive. Originally whisky was a minimum of 43%, gin 47%, and vodka was often 45 or 50%. In my opinion the higher strengths taste better.

Legislation - Freedom of the press

This book is permitted to be read and sold in democratic countries with freedom of the press. Once again it must be pointed out that the contents of this book do not comprise an invitation to put into practice anything that is unlawful in the country of the reader. The reader is urged to follow the current laws that apply where he or she lives.

It is obvious

It should be obvious that this book is neither a dare nor a challenge to the reader to engage in distillation of spirits if it is considered an unlawful offence by the legal administration in which he or she resides in. Surely there is no one who seriously believes that?

Home distillation is a current topic of discussion in many countries, and such knowledge is a light burden. This book imparts knowledge that makes intelligent discussion even more pleasant.

Punishment

In countries where it is unlawful to read this book, to make spirits or to own distillation apparatus, the above can happen if one breaks the law.

Is the law wrong in your country?

If amateur distillation for your own use is prohibited in your country, and in your opinion this is wrong, tell your politicians. Mail them, phone them, write to newspapers, or make a homepage. Work democratically. But do not break the law. Try to change it instead.

Internet Links -
Here are some great links for the Internet.

The Amazing Still - so simple that it is sheer genius! The Amazing Still needs no stove or cooling water. It is legal to own in most countries, is very affordable, and can be built in 15 minutes:
www.amazingstill.com

A good immersion heater (often hard to find locally) for The Amazing Still:
www.allfreightfree.com/homebrewing/immersion-heater.html

For info about pot distilling (grappa, and fruit brandy):
www.schnaps.co.at

Calculator for alcohol mixing and dilution:
www.distillery-yeast.com/distillery-tips/converters/#blanda_alkohol

For real whisky yeast with AG to improve the whisky:
www.whiskeyyeast.com

Absinthe extract, all natural, makes great absinthe:
www.absintheliquor.com

For purchase of a great table top air cooled still:
www.easystill.com

For more info about Turbo Yeast:
www.turbo-yeast.com

For super quality turbo yeast, essences, activated carbon, Raschig rings, instruments, and more:
www.partymanshop.com

Make your own wine labels on your computer; very nice and inexpensive:
www.homewinelabels.com

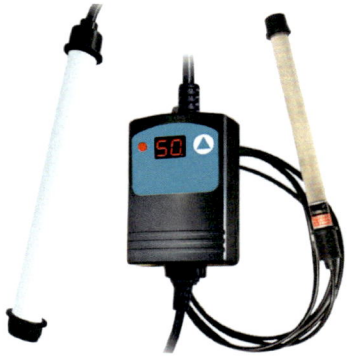

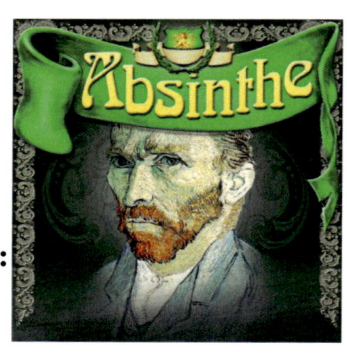

Free🍒Labelmaker.com

Make your own personalised wine and liquor labels online - it is free!
www.freelabelmaker.com

For info about Raschig rings: www.raschig-rings.com

**Free drafts to build your own still: two to choose from.
These stills are as good as the Lab-master in this book and others:**
www.moonshine-still.com

Artisan Distilling - A Guide for Small Distilleries by professor Berglund worth hundreds of dollars, you can download it for FREE!
www.books24-7.com/artisan-distilling-a-guide-for-small-distilleries.html

How to build Fuel Ethanol stills, handbook:
www.books24-7.com/fuel-ethanol-stills.html

If you have a distillery, you can increase production and quality without investment. Ferment faster and to higher alcohol levels, reducing a lot of different costs: www.distillery-yeast.com

Want to run your car on alcohol fuel? Here is a great link:
www.running_on_alcohol.tripod.com

**Make a Fuel Ethanol Still using an oil drum as the boiler:
3 FREE drafts!**

www.distillery-yeast.com/distillery-tips/fuel-ethanol/fuel-still-1

www.distillery-yeast.com/distillery-tips/fuel-ethanol/fuel-still-2

www.distillery-yeast.com/distillery-tips/fuel-ethanol/fuel-still-3

Boiling point calculator for 95 % alcohol and also for water (boiling point changes with elevation): www.partyman.se/calculator.html

Different alcohol related calculators and converters:
www.distillery-yeast.com/distillery-tips/converters

Hydrometer info: for Specific Gravity hydrometers, and Oechsle Scale hydrometers. Great info! www.thehydrometer.com

Notes:

Made in the USA
Lexington, KY
10 November 2018